Read and write Russian script

Daphne West

D1432387

The author would like to thank Elena Kelly and Tracy Walsh for their help in the preparation of this book and Tatyana Izmailova for her constant support.

For UK order enquiries: please contact Bookpoint Ltd, 130 Milton Park, Abingdon, Oxon OX14 4SB. *Telephone:* +44 (0) 1235 827720. *Fax:* +44 (0) 1235 400454. Lines are open 09.00–17.00, Monday to Saturday, with a 24-hour message answering service. Details about our titles and how to order are available at www.teachyourself.com

For USA order enquiries: please contact McGraw-Hill Customer Services, PO Box 545, Blacklick, OH 43004-0545, USA. *Telephone:* 1-800-722-4726. *Fax:* 1-614-755-5645.

For Canada order enquiries: please contact McGraw-Hill Ryerson Ltd, 300 Water St, Whitby, Ontario L1N 9B6, Canada. *Telephone:* 905 430 5000. *Fax:* 905 430 5020.

Long renowned as the authoritative source for self-guided learning – with more than 50 million copies sold worldwide – the *Teach Yourself* series includes over 500 titles in the fields of languages, crafts, hobbies, business, computing and education.

British Library Cataloguing in Publication Data: a catalogue record for this title is available from the British Library.

Library of Congress Catalog Card Number: on file.

First published in UK 2000 by Hodder Education, part of Hachette UK, 338 Euston Road, London NW1 3BH as Beginner's Russian Script.

First published in US 2000 by The McGraw-Hill Companies, Inc.

This edition published 2010.

The *Teach Yourself* name is a registered trade mark of Hachette UK.

Copyright © 2000, 2003, 2010 Daphne West

In UK: All rights reserved. Apart from any permitted use under UK copyright law, no part of this publication may be reproduced or transmitted in any form or by any means, electronic or mechanical, including photocopy, recording, or any information, storage and retrieval system, without permission in writing from the publisher or under licence from the Copyright Licensing Agency Limited. Further details of such licences (for reprographic reproduction) may be obtained from the Copyright Licensing Agency Limited, of Saffron House, 6–10 Kirby Street, London EC1N 8TS.

In US: All rights reserved. Except as permitted under the United States Copyright Act of 1976, no part of this publication may be reproduced or distributed in any form or by any means, or stored in a database or retrieval system, without the prior written permission of the publisher.

Typeset by MPS Limited, A Macmillan Company.

Printed in Great Britain for Hodder Education, an Hachette UK Company, 338 Euston Road, London NW1 3BH, by CPI Cox & Wyman, Reading, Berkshire, RG1 8EX.

The publisher has used its best endeavours to ensure that the URLs for external websites referred to in this book are correct and active at the time of going to press. However, the publisher and the author have no responsibility for the websites and can make no guarantee that a site will remain live or that the content will remain relevant, decent or appropriate.

Hachette UK's policy is to use papers that are natural, renewable and recyclable products and made from wood grown in sustainable forests. The logging and manufacturing processes are expected to conform to the environmental regulations of the country of origin.

Impression number 10 9 8 7 6 5 4 3 2 1

Year 2014 2013 2012 2011 2010

Contents

....

Credits

Front cover: © Oxford Illustrators.

Back cover: © Jakub Semeniuk/iStockphoto.com, © Royalty-Free/
Corbis, © agencyby/iStockphoto.com, © Andy Cook/iStockphoto.
com, © Christopher Ewing/iStockphoto.com, © zebicho – Fotolia.
com, © Geoffrey Holman/iStockphoto.com, © Photodisc/Getty
Images, © James C. Pruitt/iStockphoto.com, © Mohamed Saber –
Fotolia.com

Meet the author

My passion for Russian began when it was offered at my school as an alternative to O-level Physics. At the University of Durham I gained a first-class honours degree in Russian with distinction in spoken Russian, followed by a PhD on the poet Mandelshtam. I have taught in schools and further education colleges; I was Head of Modern Languages at Sherborne School for Girls and Sevenoaks School, and Headmistress of the Maynard School in Exeter. I have been Chief Examiner for GCSE and A-level Russian, and my publications include three titles in this series, as well as A-level textbooks (*Poshli dalshe, Tranzit, Kompas*). In 1993 I was awarded the Pushkin Medal by the Pushkin Insitute, Moscow, for contributions to the teaching of Russian. In the early 1990s I established an exchange which has flourished for nearly twenty years with School No.7 in Perm (a city in the Urals closed to foreigners in Soviet times). I am now a freelance teacher and writer, and my former Russian students include teachers of Russian in schools and universities, as well those who have made their careers in Russia working for businesses and charitable organisations. In January 2010 I became the editor of *Rusistika*, the Russian journal of the Association of Language Learning.

Daphne West

Only got a minute?

Russian is one of the most commonly spoken languages in the world: approximately 270 million speak it worldwide, with just over 140 million living in the Russian Federation.

Russian is a Slavonic language which belongs to the same Indo-European family as English. It has been influenced by a range of languages, including Old Church Slavonic, English, French, German, Hebrew, Latin and Greek. Russian uses the Cyrillic alphabet (named after the ninth-century monk St Cyril, its reputed creator); the Cyrillic alphabet has 33 letters.

Can you learn Russian without learning the Cyrillic alphabet? Only at the very basic level of being able to understand a few spoken words. To use the language to any extent at all (even just to recognize street signs), you need to know the alphabet.

Is the alphabet difficult to learn? It certainly needs practice, but it is not completely different from English. Some letters look and sound like their English equivalents:

the letters **T**, **A** and **M**, for example, spell the word там, which means *there*. Some letters look familiar to the English speaker, but they sound different: e.g. **E** is pronounced like 'ye' in the word *yet*, **P** like 'r' in *rat* (though rolled), so **театр**, which means *theatre*, is pronounced tyeatr. A third group of letters do not look like English letters; some are connected with Greek, such as **Ф** (which sounds like 'f' in *far*), and others cannot be rendered by one English letter – **Ш** is pronounced 'sh' – and the word **шарф** means *scarf*.

This course concentrates on the printed alphabet, but also gives you the opportunity to practise the handwritten version.

Pronunciation in Russian is straightforward: if you pronounce each letter individually, you will produce the whole word, i.e. the spelling represents the sound, which is not always the case in English (think of *draft* and *draught*, for example).

Learning the alphabet is your first step on the road to acquaintance with Russia, its language and culture.

5 Only got five minutes?

Russian is one of the six most widely spoken languages in the world, with approximately 270 million speakers. It is one of the official languages of the United Nations; just over 25% of the world's scientific literature is in Russian; and it is becoming increasingly important in the sphere of business. Russia is the largest country in the world, spreading over two continents, eleven time zones and embracing a wide variety of climatic and geographic conditions, as well as a vast wealth of natural resources. Although the Russian Federation covers an area of over 10 million square kilometres, there is a surprising degree of uniformity in the Russian spoken from St Petersburg in the far west to Vladivostok on the eastern Pacific coast. Russian is still widely spoken in countries which used to be part of the Soviet Union and which still have large Russian communities (Estonia, Kazakhstan and Ukraine, for example).

Russian is a Slavonic language which belongs to the Slavonic branch of the Indo-European family (the group of languages to which English also belongs) and it has links with Dutch, English, French, German, Latin and Greek, as well as with Old Church Slavonic.

The first striking difference between English and Russian is that Russian uses the Cyrillic alphabet (named after the ninth-century monk St Cyril, its reputed creator.) Knowledge of the alphabet is the essential first building block in your study of Russian (and gives you immediate independence when in Russia – you can read the street signs!). It is possible to transliterate Russian words (i.e. produce an approximation of their sound by using English letters), but this can be very time consuming – sometimes we need as many as four English letters to produce the sound of one Russian letter; more importantly, it is not helpful to rely on transliteration if you want to learn the alphabet!

There are 33 letters in the Russian alphabet, which is made up of the same sort of components as the English alphabet (consonants and vowels, plus a couple of letters which have no sound of their own but which affect the sound of other letters). The aim of this course is to give you a gradual introduction to the printed alphabet, with plenty of practice in recognizing contemporary Russian words, as well as a few very basic facts about Russian grammar, and some information about Russian life and culture. The emphasis is very much on printed Cyrillic, but you are also introduced to the written ('cursive') script. Many of the words used, particularly in the opening units, are 'cognates', i.e. their sound is similar to and means the same thing as their English equivalents.

One group of letters in the Cyrillic alphabet look and sound like their English counterparts: **А**, **О**, **К**, **М**, **Т** – so, for example, **атом** means *atom*.

Some letters look familiar to the English speaker, but they sound different, e.g. **Е** is pronounced like 'ye' in the word *yet*, **Н** like 'n' in *next*, **Р** like 'r' in *rat* (though rolled), and **С** like 's' in *set*. So, **нос** means *nose*, **сорт** means *sort/variety*, **стерео** means *stereo*, and **трек** is a *track* (either sports or musical).

A third group of letters do not look like English letters, but sound familiar; some are connected with Greek, such as **П** (sounds like 'p' in *pat*) and **Ф** (sounds like 'f' in *far*). So, **портрет** means *portrait*, and **факт** means *fact*.

A fourth group of letters cannot be rendered by one English letter. For example, **ш** is pronounced 'sh' – and the word **шапка** means *hat* or *cap*.

Some learners of Russian think at first that the alphabet looks as if it has been written backwards. This is principally because of the vowels **И** (pronounced 'ee' as in *feet*) and **Я** (pronounced 'ya' as in *yak*). The names of many countries feature both of these letters, e.g **Япония** (*Japan*) and **Испания** (*Spain*). **Э** is pronounced like the 'e' in *let*, so **эксперт** means *expert* – in Russian this letter is called a 'backwards e'.

Pronunciation in Russian is straightforward: if you pronounce each letter individually, you will produce the whole word, i.e. the spelling represents the sound, which is not always the case in English (think of *bought* and *bough*, for example). Stress (which part of the word is emphasized) is an important feature of Russian pronunciation. No matter how many syllables there are in a word, only one of them can be stressed; in this course the stressed vowel is underlined, e.g. **эксперт**, **Яп<u>о</u>ния**.

Russian vocabulary, and particularly that relating to the media, entertainment and technology, has been greatly influenced in recent years by the vocabulary of Western European languages (especially English), so luckily there is now a rich pool of cognates. Examples of this in music are the words **поп** (*pop*), **рок** (*rock*) and **рэп** (*rap*).

Once equipped with the alphabet, you will be able to develop the skills of reading and writing, and they will in turn help you make progress with your spoken and listening skills. Knowledge of the language will give you greater access to the rich world of Russian life and culture. Russia's history, which begins with the founding of Kievan Rus' in the tenth century (the time of the first examples of written Russian), is studded with dramatic and tumultuous events and colourful characters. Its culture is vast and varied, and includes some of the world's greatest writers (e.g. Chekhov, Dostoevsky, Gogol, Mandelshtam, Pushkin, Tolstoy, Turgenev) and composers (e.g. Prokofiev, Shostakovich, Stravinsky, Tchaikovsky), as well as some of the finest exponents of ballet, chess, opera, painting, film and sport – all linked by what Turgenev called the 'great, powerful, true and free Russian language!'.

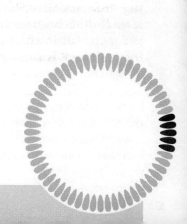

10 Only got ten minutes?

According to the great 18th-century Russian scientist and writer Mikhail Lomonosov, the Russian language has 'the magnificence of Spanish, the vivacity of French, the strength of German, the tenderness of Italian, and, on top of all that, the richness and strong, concise description of Greek and Latin'. Quite a recommendation!

The study of the Russian language can indeed be an enriching experience in itself, and a knowledge of the language opens doors to the infinite variety of Russian life and culture.

One of the official languages of the United Nations, Russian is spoken by approximately 270 million people worldwide, with about 140 million living in the Russian Federation. It is the most widespread of the Slavonic languages and is still widely spoken in countries which used to be part of the Soviet Union and still have large Russian communities (Estonia, Kazakhstan and Ukraine, for example). More than 25% of the world's scientific literature is in Russian.

The Russian Federation straddles Europe and Asia, but Russian, like English, belongs to the Indo-European family of languages. It developed from Eastern Slavic, a language spoken by Slavs who migrated eastwards after the seventh century BC. Although the roots of the Russian language lie in Old East Slavonic and Old Church Slavonic, it has also been influenced by Classical Greek, Latin, Dutch, English, French and German. Russian's closest relatives, in the spoken language at least, are Belorussian and Ukrainian.

How important is it to learn Russian for the purposes of business, travel and tourism? And what about literature, music, theatre and sport? Whilst it is true that in most major Russian cities there are excellent speakers of English in all these spheres, it is certainly not the case that English is spoken widely everywhere. Russians understand that their language is often viewed as 'difficult', so the effort by visitors to speak Russian is greatly appreciated. An ability to understand and communicate, even at a basic level, can enhance a tourist's enjoyment and understanding of their visit, and enable more effective relations in the business context, for example.

So how difficult a language is Russian? For the English speaker, it is less straightforward initially (particularly from the point of view of vocabulary) than Western European languages such as French, German, Italian and Spanish. However, Russian shares a significant amount of vocabulary and grammatical structures with modern Western European languages, as well as with Classical Greek and Latin, which means that students encounter lots of reassuringly familiar items as their study progresses.

The first important task when beginning the study of Russian is to learn the Cyrillic alphabet: without knowledge of the alphabet it is not possible to proceed beyond the most basic comprehension … and you can't even read the street signs! Although it is possible to 'transliterate' Russian words (i.e. give approximations of their sound using English letters), this can be time-consuming and unhelpful; time-consuming because some Cyrillic letters need up to four English letters to render them, and unhelpful in learning and developing the skills of reading and writing in Russian.

The Cyrillic alphabet is named after the ninth-century monk St Cyril, its reputed creator. It was influenced primarily by Greek, with extra letters created to represent Slavonic sounds. The first examples of written Russian date from the tenth century, after which the alphabet developed various forms up to the reign of Peter the Great in the eighteenth century, when the alphabet was regularized; after the Revolution in 1917, the alphabet was further 'tidied up' and unnecessary characters were dispensed with, leaving the alphabet as we have it today. Learning the Cyrillic alphabet is not a daunting task because it has so much in common with the Latin alphabet (as used in English), whilst some letters may be familiar already (via Greek and mathematics); and those letters created to represent sounds specific to Russian are so intriguing that it is difficult <u>not</u> to remember them!

There are 33 letters to be learnt. This course introduces you gradually to the printed alphabet, with lots of practice, some information about very basic grammar points and also about Russian life and culture. The handwritten (or cursive) alphabet is also introduced, but the main emphasis is on the printed form of Cyrillic. The letters are introduced in groups, with words being built up gradually from the letters met.

- So, for example, the following letters look and sound like their English counterparts: the letters **К Т О** give the Russian word for *who*. The Cyrillic letters **Т А М** give the word for *there*.
- Some letters look familiar but sound different, e.g. **Н** sounds like the English letter 'n', and **С** sounds like the English letter 's' – so the Russian for *nose* is **нос**.
- Students of Greek or Mathematics will recognize the Cyrillic **П** as Pi and **Ф** as Phi. So, **пакт** is a *pact*, and **факс** is a *fax*.
- Amongst the intriguingly different characters is the beautiful letter **Ж** (pronounced 'zh'), as in the word **нож** (meaning *knife*); and the letter **Ц** gives the 'ts' sound which starts the Russian word for *tsar*.
- There are two letters which may look as if they are 'backwards' to you: **И** (pronounced 'ee', as in *feet*) and **Я** (pronounced 'ya' as in *yak*). These two letters often occur in the names of countries – for example, **Франция** (*France*) and **Россия** (*Russia*).

Pronunciation in Russian is achieved simply by pronouncing each letter individually, i.e. words sound as they are spelt; this makes Russian pronunciation a good deal easier than English, where very often a word is not pronounced as it is written (e.g. *cough*) or may mean different things when pronounced differently (e.g. 'Have you *read* this book? It's a good *read*.')

A very important feature of Russian pronunciation is stress: no matter how many syllables there are in a Russian word, only one of them can be emphasized. To achieve authentic pronunciation it is very important to get the stress right – just think how strange it would sound in English if you emphasized the first syllable of the word *event* instead of the second. In this course, the stressed syllable is indicated by underlining of the vowel to be emphasized – for example, **Фр<u>а</u>нция** (*France*) and **Росс<u>и</u>я** (*Russia*).

Characteristic of the 'sound' of Russian is its system of 'hard' and 'soft' vowels. So, for example, Russian has both the 'hard' sounding vowel **А** (which sounds like the English 'a' in *far*) and **Я** which is pronounced like the letters 'ya' in *yak*. 'Soft' vowels 'soften' (or 'palatalize') the consonants which precede them. This may sound complicated, but it is not unlike English: try saying these two words and listen to the difference caused by the hard 'oo' sound and the soft 'u':

Hard: moon   Soft: music

And in Russian:

Hard: **да** (which means *yes*)   Soft: **дядя** (which means *uncle*).

In recent years Russian vocabulary has been increasingly influenced by Western European culture. The influence of English words is particularly strong in the spheres of business, the media and entertainment, sport, the Internet and computer technology. For example, the words for goalkeeper (**голк<u>и</u>пер** – pronounced 'golk<u>ee</u>pyer') and half time (**х<u>а</u>втайм** – pronounced 'khaftayim') are clearly straight from English.

Russia is the largest country in the world, spreading over two continents, eleven time zones and embracing a wide variety of climatic and geographic conditions, as well as a vast wealth of natural resources. Although the Russian Federation covers an area of over 10 million square kilometres, there is a surprising degree of uniformity in the Russian spoken from St Petersburg in the far west to Vladivostok on the eastern Pacific coast.

Russia is not only the largest country in the world (with the longest continuous railway on earth – the Trans-Siberian), but it has an astonishingly rich history and culture. Its history, which begins with the founding of Kievan Rus' in the tenth century, is studded with tumultuous events, and dramatic characters, among them: Ivan the Terrible, Peter the Great, Catherine the Great, Rasputin, Lenin, Trotsky and Stalin – to name but a few. Its literature is vast and varied, and includes some of the world's greatest writers (e.g. Chekhov, Dostoevsky, Gogol, Mandelshtam, Pushkin, Tolstoy, Turgenev) and composers (e.g. Borodin, Glinka, Prokofiev, Rimsky-Korsakov, Shostakovich, Stravinsky, Tchaikovsky), as well as some of the finest exponents of ballet (Pavlova, Nureyev, Nijinsky, Diaghilev), chess (Karpov, Kasparov), film (Eisenstein, Sokurov, Tarkovsky), painting (Goncharova, Larionov, Levitan, Rublyov, Repin), mathematics and science (Bugayev, Kovalevskaya, Mendeleyev, Pavlov, Sakharov, Zhukovsky), sport (from figure skating to football, ice hockey to gymnastics) and theatre (Stanislavsky, Meyerhold). No wonder the nineteenth-century poet Tyutchev said that Russia could not be 'measured with a standard yardstick'! Learning the alphabet is your first step on the road to acquaintance with Russia, its language and culture.

Introduction

Read and write Russian script is the course to use if you are a complete beginner who wants to learn the Russian alphabet, or if your knowledge of Russian has become rusty and you need to refamiliarize yourself with the alphabet. The purpose of this book is to present the letters gradually, giving lots of practice and revision sections, so that by the end of the course you will feel able to read and to write Russian script. This course will get you started and give you the confidence to move on to study other aspects of the language (listening, speaking and grammar).

Russian script – how 'different' is it?

The complete beginner can sometimes feel that Russian might be rather difficult to learn because the script initially looks very different. Russian is from the same family of languages as English (Indo-European) and has been very much influenced by languages such as Latin and French, but also by Classical Greek, Hebrew and Old Church Slavonic. In the 9th century a monk called St Cyril is reputed to have devised the Russian script – hence its name: *Cyrillic*. It is possible to transliterate Russian words (i.e. produce an approximation of their sound by using English letters), but this can be very time consuming – sometimes we need as many as four English letters to produce the sound of one Russian letter. Thanks to St Cyril there are only 33 letters in the Russian alphabet, and it is made up of the same sort of components as the English alphabet (consonants and vowels, plus a couple of letters which have no sound of their own but affect the sound of other letters). So the Russian script has got quite a lot in common with English! And remember – Russian really is much simpler once you know the script. Of course, if you are going to visit Russia, you need a basic recognition of the script, at least to be able to read the street signs and find your way around. The handwritten alphabet is a little different from the printed version – you will be meeting both forms in this book, though the emphasis is more on the printed alphabet.

How the units work

There are ten units. In the first four units the printed alphabet will be introduced in manageable chunks of between five and twelve letters, which will be explained and practised one by one. In these units each new Russian word will also be transliterated so that you can practise saying the words as well as reading and writing them. The fifth unit will concentrate on revision of everything covered in the first four units. In Units 6 and 7 you will learn how to read and write the handwritten Russian script; it is very useful to be able to recognize this (it is often used 'decoratively' in advertisements, for example), and it is actually much quicker to write using this script than copying the form of printed letters. Finally, in Units 8 to 10 you will be given practice with words on specific topics, to give you a real sense of building your vocabulary, as well as reinforcing your knowledge of both alphabets.

Within the units you will find:

- a list of things you can expect to learn
- key facts about pronunciation, spelling and cultural information
- examples of words using the new letters
- exercises for you to practise your new knowledge (answers will be found in the Key)
- English transliterations of the Russian words and phrases.
- In the course of each unit you will find 'author insight boxes' with tips to help you understand and remember essential or tricky points, as well as additional practice in reading Russian words.
- The final part of each unit will give you opportunities to test yourself on your overall understanding of the unit, with points to remember and questions to help you.

The printed alphabet (1)

In this unit you will learn to recognize
- **Two vowels**
- **Three consonants**

You will find the letters in this unit reassuringly familiar, as they look and sound very much like their English counterparts. Remember that the most important thing in this unit is to learn to recognize and read the five letters (don't worry at this stage about learning vocabulary).

New letters: two vowels

The vowel A, a

This is pronounced like *a* in f*a*ther.

small	а
capital	А

Just by learning this letter you already know how to say several different things, because in Russian **a** means:

Letter	Meaning
а	and
а	but
а!	ah!
а?	'I'll post it now, ***shall I?***'
	'Ring me tomorrow, ***would you?***'

The vowel O, o

small	o
capital	O

This is pronounced like *o* in b*o*re.

This letter also has meanings of its own:

Letter	Meaning
o	*He's thinking **of/about** Moscow.*
o	*I hit my hand **on/against** the wall.*
o!	***Oh** no!*

If we join the two vowels together, we get the initials which stand for *joint-stock company* (a bit like the English *plc*): **AO**.

> ### Insight
> It is helpful to say out loud each Russian word you meet (even when the letters look the same and sound the same as their English counterparts). Saying new words out loud is even more important when you meet letters which look the same but sound different (in Unit 2).

New letters: three consonants

The consonant K, к

small	к
capital	K

This is pronounced like *k* in *k*ite.

We can use the vowel **a** with this letter to make a very common word:

Letter	Russian word	Meaning
к	как	how (as in 'How are you?') as/like (as in 'I did as you asked.') what! (as in 'What?! Forgotten again?!')

Remember that by making the sound of each individual letter, you get the sound of the whole word. So try that now: к + а + к = как.

Russian has some magnificently picturesque proverbs and sayings, many of which involve the word KAK. For example, the Russian equivalent of *like a bolt from the blue* is *like snow onto your head* (see Unit 3 for the Russian version of this!).

The consonant M, м

This is pronounced like *m* in *m*otor.

small	М
capital	М

We can use the vowel **a** with this letter to make a word (although it's rather less common than как!):

Letter	Russian word	Meaning
м	мак	poppy

Remember that by making the sound of each individual letter, you get the sound of the whole word. So try that now: м + а + к = мак.

The letters K-O-M spell the Russian word for 'lump' or 'ball'; this word is used in another picturesque Russian proverb which literally means *the first pancake is always a lump* – the equivalent of *practice makes perfect* (see Unit 4 for the Russian version of this!)

The consonant T, т

This is pronounced like *t* in *ti*red.

small	т
capital	T

We can use the vowel **a** with this letter to make two very common words:

Letter	Russian word	Meaning
т	так	*so, thus*
т	там	*there*

Remember that by making the sound of each individual letter, you get the sound of the whole word. So try that now: т + а + к = так; т + а + м = там.

Stress

So far we have met words of one syllable. If a Russian word has more than one syllable, it is important to know which syllable to 'stress' – i.e. which syllable to emphasize clearly. For example, in the Russian word for *mummy* there are two syllables. Look in the table to see which one to stress. The underlined vowel in the Russian word shows you that the first syllable is the one to emphasize (this is represented in the 'sound' column by the vowel in **bold** and <u>underlined</u>):

Russian word	Sound	Meaning
м**а**ма	m**a**ma	*mummy*

The good news is that you never need to mark the stress when you are writing in Russian – it's just underlined in this course to help you while you are learning. Of course, Russian isn't the only language where emphasis is important. In English, emphasizing the wrong part of the word can sometimes change the meaning (think of r**e**cord and rec**o**rd, and there is a large number of words where it would sound decidedly odd if we emphasized each syllable equally (think how we emphasize the first syllable of **e**ver, **e**verything and **fa**ther and 'throw away' the second, or the second and third). This is what happens in Russian: pronounce the stressed syllable clearly and deliberately, but skim over the others, underplay them – don't give them any emphasis (much as we deal with, for example, the last syllable, -er, of **e**ver). Try this with the Russian word for *attack*:

Russian word	Sound	Meaning
ат**а**ка	at**a**ka	*attack*

The stress mark is perhaps most important when we are dealing with words which feature the letter **o**. If the **o** is in a word of only one syllable, then it will be pronounced as described above, like *o* in b*o*re:

Russian word	Sound	Meaning
КОТ	kot	*cat*

If a word has more than one syllable and it contains an *o* which is stressed, it will always be pronounced like the *o* in b*o*re. If, however, you see a word with more than one syllable which contains an *o* without a stress mark, 'throw it away' – pronounce it like the *a* in the English word sof*a*. Practise the words in the table, which gives you examples of stressed and unstressed *o*.

Russian word	Sound	Meaning
МОТ<u>О</u>К	mat<u>o</u>k	*skein* (e.g. of wool)
<u>А</u>ТОМ	<u>a</u>tam	*atom*

Insight

Always practise saying Russian words out loud as you meet them. By making the sound of each individual letter, you get the sound of the whole word, which makes it a lot easier than English with its complicated spellings (e.g. *bough/ enough*).

Exercise 1.1

Over to you! Practise using the five letters we have just looked at by matching up the descriptions on the left with the Russian words on the right. Which goes with which? Say the Russian words out loud to help you work out the answers.

1 A physicist would be interested in this. **a** такт
2 Someone allergic to cats would avoid this. **b** а̲том
3 A diplomat needs a lot of this! **c** кака̲о
4 A doctor would deal with one of these. **d** ко̲ма
5 You might drink this before you go to bed. **e** кот

Exercise 1.2

You have already met all except one of the following words. Find the new word and you will also find out the name of a very large river which is particularly important in the Urals. All the words are in capitals, so there's no clue to help you!

1 КАК 4 МА̲МА
2 ТАМ 5 КА̲МА
3 КОТ 6 МАК

Exercise 1.3

Cover up the middle column and try reading the words in the left-hand column. How many did you get right first time?

Russian word	Sound	Meaning
акт	akt	*ceremony; formal document*
а̲том	a̲tam	*atom*
кот	kot	*cat*
кто	kto	*who*

Insight

Make yourself at home with Russian script! By covering up the transliterated versions of Russian words, you can check that you really do recognize each letter. This is something you will be asked to do in the first four units.

Exercise 1.4

Now for a real conversation – from just five letters! Can you work out what is being said?

Russian	Sound
A Кто там?	**A** Kto tam?
B Том, Мак.	**B** Tom, Mak.
A Как?! Том, Мак?!	**A** Kak?! Tom, Mak?!

1 What question are the two Scotsmen, Tom and Mac, being asked by A?

2 Is A surprised?

When you've checked your answers in the Key, try covering up the list on the right and practise saying the conversation on the left. (Did you spot that one Scotsman has a name which in Russian means *poppy*? – Which one?).

Exercise 1.5

Choose the right word from the box (you might need to look back through the unit to track all these words down).

1 You want to find out how someone is.

2 You want to say that something is there.

3 You want to find out who is there.

4 You want to say that it is so hot.

как	кто
там	так

Insight

If you wanted to say *or else/otherwise* in Russian (e.g. *Hurry up, or else you'll miss the bus!*), you would need just two words made up of three of the letters we have learnt so far: а то.

End-of-unit review – things to remember, tips and questions

(Answers to the questions are in the Key.)

1 There are 33 letters in the Cyrillic alphabet: you now know 5 of them: A, O, K, M, T.

2 One of the straightforward things about Russian is that words are usually pronounced exactly as they are written: make the sound of each letter and you get the sound of the whole word.

3 Stress: if a Russian word has more than one syllable, it is important in terms of both pronunciation and grammar to know which syllable is 'stressed'.

4 Sometimes a word can have several meanings; in Exercise 1.1 you met the word такт – a quality much needed by a diplomat. Musicians need to know this word too, since it also means *time* (in the sense of rhythm – *to beat time*) and *a bar* (in musical notation).

5 In Exercise 1.2 you met the name of a major river in the Urals – Кама. The name of two other Russian rivers can be made from our first five Russian letters: Ока is the name of a river which flows through central Russia (one of the largest tributaries of the Volga) and it is also the name of a Siberian river (a tributary of the Angara).

6 Which Russian letter can mean *and* or *but*?

7 You've had an unpleasant surprise; which Russian letter would enable you to say *Oh, no!?*

8 If you wanted to ask the question *who?*, which Russian word would you need?

9 If you wanted to explain to someone that the hotel is *there*, which Russian word would you need?

10 If you wanted to ask a question beginning with the word *how?*, which Russian word would you need?

2

The printed alphabet (2)

In this unit you will
* *Meet two more vowels and five more consonants*
* *Practise the letters learnt in Unit 1*

The fun starts here! You will find the new letters reassuringly familiar to look at, but they sound rather different from their English lookalikes. By the end of the unit we'll already be over one third of the way through the Cyrillic alphabet.

New letters: two vowels

The vowel E, e

This is pronounced like *ye* in *yet*.

small	e
capital	E

If we combine this new vowel with some of the letters we learnt in Unit 1, we get the following words:

Letter	Russian word	Sound	Meaning
e	коме́та	kam**ye**ta	*comet*
e	те́ма	t**ye**ma	*theme*

The vowel У, у

small   y
capital   У

This is pronounced like *oo* in sh*oo*t.

Here it is in combination with other letters we have met:

Letter	Russian word	Sound	Meaning
у	а**у**!	a**oo**!	*Hey!* (calling for someone's attention)
у	**у**т	toot	*here*
у	**у**тка	**oo**tka	*duck*

New letters: five consonants

The consonant В, в

small   в
capital   В

This is pronounced like *v* in *v*isit.

Here it is in combination with other letters we have met:

Letter	Russian word	Sound	Meaning
в	а**в**томат	a**v**tam**a**t	*automatic machine*
в	**в**акуум*	**v**a**koo-oom**	*vacuum*

*Remember: pronounce each letter 'y'!

Insight

We now have all the letters needed for the very common Russian word **вот**, whose basic meaning is *here/there is/are*.

Вот кот.	*Here/there is the cat.*

And with two words we met in Unit 1:

Вот как!	*Really?* (expressing surprise)
Вот так!	*That's right! That's it!*

The consonant Н, н

This is pronounced like *n* in *n*ovel.

small	н
capital	Н

Here it is in combination with other letters we have met:

Letter	Russian word	Sound	Meaning
н	мом**е**нт	mam**ye**nt	*moment*
н	нок**а**ут	nak**a**oot	*knockout*

Exercise 2.1

Over to you! Cover up the list on the right. The list on the left contains two common Russian first names, the name of an Austrian city and the river which flows through Saint Petersburg. What is the name of the river? When you've answered the question, have a look at the list on the right to check your reading of the script.

	Russian	Sound
1	А̲нна	**A**nna
2	В̲е̲на	V**ye**na
3	Нева̲	Nyev**a**
4	Анто̲н	Ant**o**n

Insight

Two common words starting with the letter **H**:

но   *but* – Used when a contradiction is being made, e.g.
       He wants to go to the theatre, but I said no. (In Unit
       1 we met A, which means *and/but*, e.g. *I like fish,
       and/but he prefers meat.*)

нет   *no*

The consonant P, p

small	p
capital	P

This letter is like *r* in *r*at but rolled (as in Italian).

Here it is in combination with the other letters we have met:

Letter	Russian word	Sound	Meaning
p	тр**е**нер	tr**ye**nyer	*coach, trainer*
p	**а**втор*	**a**vtar	*author*

*Remember that an unstressed **o** is pronounced like the a in sofa.

Exercise 2.2

Over to you! These Russian words are all to do with sport. See if you can read them. Cover up the 'sound' column and the 'meaning' column until you have finished reading the word in Russian. Two of the words should look familiar – we've met them already in this unit.

Russian word	Sound	Meaning
карт	kart	*go-kart*
нок**а**ут	nak**a**oot	*knockout*
рак**е**тка	rak**ye**tka	*racket*
трек	tryek	*track*
тр**е**нер	tr**ye**nyer	*coach, trainer*

The consonant С, с

This is pronounced like *s* in *s*ip.

small	с
capital	С

Here it is in combination with other letters we have met:

Letter	Russian word	Sound	Meaning
с	Москв**а***	Maskv**a**	*Moscow*
с	сестр**а**	syestr**a**	*sister*

*Another unstressed **o** in this word.

Insight

Remember to pronounce the words out loud. Try the following words, which are all to do with money:

к**а**сса *cash desk, till, checkout*

мон**е**та *coin* (Remember: the 'o' will sound like the 'a' in *sofa* here, because it's not stressed.)

с**у**мма *sum*

Exercise 2.3

Over to you! Here are the names of some Russian towns and rivers, but each one has a missing letter; the English version and pronunciation are given in the right-hand columns. Fill in the missing Russian letters.

Russian word	Sound	English version
1 Му__манск	M**oo**rmansk	*Murmansk*
2 Н__в**а**	Nyev**a**	*Neva*
3 Омс__	Omsk	*Omsk*
4 Москв__	Maskv**a**	*Moscow*

Now write the missing letters in the order 1–4 and you will have the Russian word for 'river':   **5** RIVER = <u>ра</u> _ _

....

Insight

The word **ум** may be short, but it has a whole range of meanings: *mind*, *intellect*, *cleverness*, *wit*, *reason*. Note some of the different ways this word can be used:

умно*	*cleverly, wisely*
не**у**мно*	*foolishly, unwisely*
с ум**о**м	*sensibly, intelligently*

* Unstressed O – pronounce it like the 'a' in *sofa*.
....

The consonant X, x

small	x
capital	X

This is pronounced like *ch* in a Scottish pronunciation of lo*ch* (in transliteration it is usually represented by *kh*).

Here it is in combination with other letters we have met:

Letter	Russian word	Sound	Meaning
x	крах	krakh	*collapse, crash* (financial)
x	характер	khar**a**ktyer	*character*

Insight

To help you practise the letter X, here are two cognates (Russian words which have approximately the same sound, as well as the same meaning, as their English equivalents):

> х**а**кер   (*computer*) *hacker*
> х**а**ос   *chaos*

Notice that X often represents the English letters 'h' or 'ch'.

More good news! In Russian there are no words for *a* or *the* (i.e. there are no indefinite or definite articles to learn), so, for example:

ресторан	(ryestar**a**n)	means either *a restaurant* or *the restaurant*
трактор	(tr**a**ktar)	means either *a tractor* or *the tractor*

Revision

We have already covered more than one third of the Cyrillic alphabet: four vowels and eight consonants.

Vowels	
a	like the *a* in *f*a*ther*
e	like *ye* in *yet*
o	like *o* in b*o*re
y	like *oo* in sh*oo*t

Consonants	
в	like *v* in *v*isit
к	like *k* in *k*ite
м	like *m* in *m*otor
н	like *n* in *n*ovel
p	like *r* in *r*at
c	like *s* in *s*ip
т	like *t* in *t*ired
x	like *ch* in lo*ch*

12 down, 21 to go!

Exercise 2.4

Time to practise our 12 letters. Match up the Russian words in the first column with their English versions in the second column. Cover up the transliterations in the third column (unless you're really stuck).

1	ресторан	**a** *chaos*	1	ryestoran
2	метро	**b** *toast*	2	myetro
3	нос	**c** *sauce*	3	nos
4	текст	**d** *thermometer*	4	tyekst
5	тост	**e** *restaurant*	5	tost
6	термометр	**f** *cosmonaut*	6	tyermomyetr
7	тон	**g** *nose*	7	ton
8	хаос	**h** *metro*	8	kha-as
9	космонавт	**i** *text*	9	kasmanavt
10	соус	**j** *tone*	10	so-oos

Exercise 2.5

Look at the descriptions on the left, then try to fill in the missing letters in the middle column. Transliterations are given in the right-hand column – try not to look at it until you've had a go at all five questions!

1 A musician would play in one	ор__естр	arkyestr
2 An actor would act in one	теат__	tyeatr
3 A fish would swim in one	р__ка	ryeka
4 A waiter would work in one	ре__торан	ryestaran
5 A farmer would drive one	трак__ор	traktar

Now write the missing letters in the order 1–5 and you will have the Russian word for cross:

6 CROSS = _ _ _ _ _

Exercise 2.6

You can compile five Russian words connected with music from the letters in the box (below). Can you find all five?

You should be able to find the Russian words for the following: note, orchestra, rock, tenor, tone.

а е к н о р с т

End-of-unit review – things to remember, tips and questions

(Answers to the questions are in the Key.)

1 There are no definite articles (*the*) or indefinite articles (*a*) in Russian.

2 E looks like the English letter, but is pronounced 'ye', as in *yet*.

3 H looks like the English letter, but it is the Russian letter for N.

4 B looks like the English letter, but it is the Russian letter for V.

5 P looks like the English letter, but it is the Russian letter for R (rolled in Russian!).

6 C looks like the English letter, but it is the Russian letter for S.

7 What is the basic meaning of the Russian word вот?

8 How do you say *no* in Russian?

9 What is the Russian word for: *cash desk, till, check out*?

10 How do you say *Moscow* in Russian?

3

The printed alphabet (3)

In this unit you will
- *Meet two more vowels and seven more consonants*
- *Practise the twelve letters learnt in Units 1 and 2*

The new letters in this unit may not look like English letters, but they do sound familiar to the English ear (and if you have studied Greek or mathematics you'll recognize some of them). By the end of this unit we will have covered almost two thirds of the Russian alphabet.

New letters: two vowels

These two vowels look very similar.

The vowel И, и

This is pronounced like *ee* in f**ee**t.

small	и
capital	И

Here it is in combination with some of the letters we met in Units 1 and 2:

Russian word	Sound	Meaning
вин**о**	veen**o**	wine
рис	rees	rice
такс**и**	taks**ee**	taxi
кин**о**	keen**o**	cinema

Exercise 3.1

Over to you! Practise using this new vowel along with the letters we have already learnt in Units 1 and 2. Here are some common Russian first names. Their transliterated versions are on the right, but they've been mixed up – sort out which goes with which:

1	Иван	**a**	K<u>ee</u>ra
2	Ир<u>и</u>на	**b**	Neek<u>ee</u>ta
3	К<u>и</u>ра	**c**	Eev<u>a</u>n
4	Ник<u>и</u>та	**d**	Eer<u>ee</u>na

When you've checked your answers in the Key, cover up the list on the right and practise saying the names.

Insight

Two occupations featuring the letter И:

ветерин**а**р	*veterinary surgeon*
т**е**хник	*technician*

The Russian verb *to be* has no present tense, and as there is also no article in Russian, all you need to say to describe people's occupations is:

Ир**и**на ветерин**а**р, а Ив**а**н т**е**хник. *Irina (is a) vet, but/ and Ivan (is a) technician.* (The brackets show you which words are not present in the Russian.)

The vowel Й, й

small	**й**
capital	**Й**

This is pronounced like *y* in b*oy*.

This is called a 'short и' (и кр**а**ткое in Russian), and 99% of the time you will find this letter following another vowel; it is used to make what in English is called a diphthong (two vowels pronounced as one syllable, like 'b*oy*', 'Th*ai*land'). It is occasionally found as the first letter of a word when Russian is trying to imitate the sound of a word from another language, e.g. it is required at the beginning of the Russian version of York: Йорк.

Here it is in combination with some of the letters we have already met in Units 1 and 2:

Russian word	Sound	Meaning
ай!	aiy!	*oh! ouch!*
Кит**ай**	Keet**aiy**	*China*
май	maiy	*May* (the month)
рай**о**н	raiy**o**n	*region*

A very short, but much used, word in Russian is ой (oiy). It expresses surprise, pain, fear or rapture. So if you're expressing surprise because you've suddenly seen Ivan and you weren't expecting to, you might say:

Ой! Вот Ив**а**н!   Oiy! Vot Eev**a**n!   *Oh! There's Ivan!*

Practise saying this, making sure you cover up the two right-hand columns.

New letters: seven consonants

The consonant Б, б

This is pronounced like *b* in *b*ox.

small	б
capital	Б

The consonant Г, г

This is pronounced like *g* in *g*oat.

small	г
capital	Г

Notice that it is a hard *g* (as in *g*et, *g*ive), never a soft *g* (as in *g*inger).

The consonant Д, д

small	д
capital	Д

This is pronounced like *d* in *d*aughter.

Here are our two new vowels and our three new consonants from this unit in combination with some of the letters we have already met in Units 1 and 2:

Russian word	Sound	Meaning
бан**а**н	ban**a**n	*banana*
таб**а**к	tab**a**k	*tobacco*
гид	geed (hard 'g'!)	*guide* (a person who shows you round)
д**о**ктор	d**o**ktar	*doctor*
аг**е**нт	ag**ye**nt	*agent*
Мадр**и**д	Madr**ee**d	*Madrid*
Андр**е**й	Andr**ye**iy	*Andrei* (a popular name for a man)

Insight

The Russian word for *he* is он; *she* is он**а**, and *they* is он**и** (the unstressed O in both он**а** and он**и** is pronounced like the 'a' in *sofa*!):

Он гид.	*He is a guide.*
Он**а** медсестр**а**.	*She is a nurse* (literally, '*medical sister*').
Он**и** т**е**хники.	*They are technicians.*

Exercise 3.2

Over to you! Practise our two new vowels and three new consonants – answer the following questions.

1 Russia's national drink is:

  a во́дка

  б ви́ски

  в вино́

2 To withdraw money, go to the:

  a теа́тр

  б дискоте́ка

  в банк

3 Which of these cities is not in England?

  a Бирминга́м

  б Гонко́нг

  в Йорк

4 Which of the following is a means of transport?

  a ра́дио

  б а́дрес

  в трамва́й

New letters: remaining four consonants

The consonant З, з

small	з
capital	З

This is pronounced like *z* in *z*oo.

The consonant Л, л

small	л
capital	Л

This is pronounced like *l* in *l*amp.

The consonant П, п

small	п
capital	П

This is pronounced like *p* in *p*each.

The consonant Ф, ф

This is pronounced like *f* in *funny*.

small	ф
capital	Ф

Here are our last four new consonants, з, л, п, and ф, in combination with some of the letters we met in Units 1 and 2:

Russian word	Sound	Meaning
зоопарк	za-apark	zoo
анализ	analeez	analysis
суп	soop	soup
паспорт	paspart	passport
футбол	footbol	football
билет	beelyet	ticket
форвард	forvard	forward (e.g. in football)
профессор	prafyessar	professor

Insight

We have now covered the letters used in some useful words which ask and tell about location:

где?	where?
далеко	a long way/far (Think of Dr Who's daleks, which came from afar!)
близко	near, close by
Где банк? Далеко?	Where's the bank? Is it far?
Нет, близко.	No, it's close by.

Revision

We have now covered two thirds of the Cyrillic alphabet – we have looked at six vowels and 15 consonants (21 down, 12 to go).

Remember to cover up the right-hand column to test yourself. How many letters can you recognize?

Vowels	
а	like the *a* in f*a*ther
е	like *ye* in *ye*t
и	like *ee* in f*ee*t
й	like *y* in bo*y*
о	like *o* in b*o*re
у	like *oo* in sh*oo*t

Consonants	
б	like *b* in *b*ank
в	like *v* in *v*isit
г	like *g* in *g*oat
д	like *d* in *d*aughter
з	like *z* in *z*oo
к	like *k* in *k*ite
л	like *l* in *l*amp
м	like *m* in *m*otor
н	like *n* in *n*ovel
п	like *p* in *p*each
р	like *r* in *r*at
с	like *s* in *s*ip
т	like *t* in *t*ired
ф	like *f* in *f*unny
х	like *ch* in lo*ch*

21 down, 12 to go!

Exercise 3.3

In the left-hand column are some common Russian first names, but each one has a letter missing. Their transliterated version is given in the right-hand column. Fill in the missing Russian letter.

1	Бори__	*Boris* (m.)	(unstressed 'o') Bar<u>ee</u>s
2	К__ра	*Kira* (f.)	K<u>ee</u>ra
3	Па__ел	*Pavel* (m.)	P<u>a</u>vyel
4	Ва__им	*Vadim* (m.)	Vad<u>ee</u>m
5	Анн__	*Anna* (f.)	<u>A</u>nna
6	Сер__ей	*Sergei* (m.)	Syerg<u>ye</u>iy
7	Свет__ана	*Svetlana* (f.)	Svyetl<u>a</u>na
8	Владими__	*Vladimir* (m.)	Vlad<u>ee</u>meer
9	Ели_ав<u>е</u>та	*Elizaveta* (f.)	Yeleezavy<u>e</u>ta
10	И_<u>а</u>н	*Ivan* (m.)	Eev<u>a</u>n

Exercise 3.4

Find the sports by using the letters from the box to fill the blanks in each word (you can use letters more than once).

а	б	в	е
й	к	л	о
с	т	у	ф

1 б _ _ к _ _ бол
2 в _ л _ _ бол
3 _ у _ бол

Exercise 3.5

Look carefully at the drawing of Vladimir's head.

ГОЛОВА ВЛАДИМИРА = the head of Vladimir

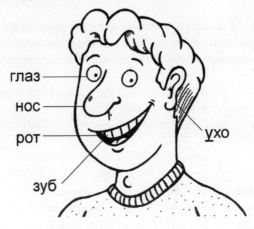

глаз
нос
рот
зуб
<u>у</u>хо

Vladimir isn't feeling well and he explains to the doctor what his symptoms are. The word болит (bal<u>ee</u>t) means *it hurts, it aches, it's painful, it's sore*. So when Vladimir wants to explain that his head aches, he says: болит голова (bal<u>ee</u>t galav<u>a</u>).

What other symptoms is he complaining of?

Russian	**Sound**
1 Ай! Бол<u>и</u>т <u>у</u>хо!	Aiy! Bal<u>ee</u>t <u>oo</u>kha!
2 Ай! Бол<u>и</u>т зуб!	Aiy! Bal<u>ee</u>t zoob!

Insight

The Russian word не is used in negative statements:

Ив<u>а</u>н дант<u>и</u>ст?	*Is Ivan a dentist?*
Нет! Он НЕ дант<u>и</u>ст, он ветерин<u>а</u>р.	*No! He's not a dentist – he's a vet.*

To be really emphatic, use the word for *yes* – да – before you say нет: ДА нет! = *certainly not!*

Exercise 3.6

Cover up the 'sound' and 'meaning' columns of each box and read the 'who/what' and 'place' words in the left-hand column. Then match up the 'who/what' words with the 'places' in the second box.

Who/what	Sound	Meaning
1 банкир	bank**ee**r	*banker*
2 йогурт	iy**o**gurt	*yoghurt*
3 форвард	f**o**rvard	*forward*
4 опера	**o**pyera	*opera*
5 тигр	teegr	*tiger*
6 принтер	pr**ee**ntyer	*printer*

Place	Sound	Meaning
a офис	**o**fees	*office*
b театр	tye**a**tr	*theatre*
c банк	bank	*bank*
d зоопарк	za-ap**a**rk	*zoo*
e стадион	stadee**o**n	*stadium*
f ресторан	ryestar**a**n	*restaurant*

For example: 1 → c: банкир → банк

Insight

In Unit 1 we met the Russian proverb which is the equivalent of *like a bolt from the blue*. We have now met all the letters needed to say this in Russian: **как снег на голову** (literally, 'like snow onto your head').

Exercise 3.7

How many of these places can you recognize? This time, there's no right-hand column to help you (but you will find the answers in the Key).

1 Америка
2 Аргентина
3 Африка
4 Мексика
5 Канада
6 Кипр
7 Куба
8 Пакистан
9 Уганда
10 Украина

End-of-unit review – things to remember, tips and questions

(Answers to the questions are in the Key.)

1 The Russian verb *to be* does not have a present tense.

2 The letter Й almost always follows a vowel (e.g. мой = *my*).

3 When you pronounce the Russian word где (*where*), be careful to pronounce the Г and Д very close together. (English is much more used to separating these two consonants with a vowel!)

4 The Russian word for *he* is он; *she* is она, and *they* is они.

5 The Russian word for *not* is не: Он не банкир. *He isn't a banker.*

6 The Russian equivalent of 'g' (Г) is always pronounced as a hard 'g' (as in *give*) and never soft (as the 'g' in *general*).

7 Something beginning with К: can you work out what the following three words mean in English?
комититет комплекс контакт

8 Something beginning with Л: can you work out what the following three words mean in English?
лаванда, лифт, литература

9 Something beginning with М: can you work out what the following three words mean in English?
мегабайт, микроб, миллион

10 Something beginning with П: can you work out what the following three words mean in English?
паразит, порт, портрет

4

The printed alphabet (4)

In this unit you will
- *Meet five more vowels, five more consonants and two 'signs' which have no sound of their own*
- *Practise all the letters of the Cyrillic alphabet*
- *Learn about Russian names*

Most of the 12 new letters in this unit look very different from the characters of the English alphabet. They sound different from English characters in the sense that more than one English letter may be needed to represent the sound of one Russian letter. We are going to meet five new vowels and five new consonants, plus two characters which have no sound of their own.

New letters: five new vowels

The vowel Ё, ё

This does not look too unusual and is pronounced like *yo* in *yo*nder.

small	ё
capital	Ё

The vowel Ы, ы

This does look unfamiliar. There is no real equivalent sound in English. With your

small	ы
capital	Ы

mouth slightly open (but not moving your lips!), draw your tongue back a little and say the English word *ill*. This letter sounds rather like the *i* of *i*ll if pronounced as described.

Insight

In Unit 1 we met the Russian proverb which is the equivalent of *practice makes perfect*. The Russian for this literally means *the first pancake is always a lump* and we have now met all the letters needed for this phrase **первый** (*first*) **блин** (*pancake*) **всегда** (*always*) **комом** (*like a lump*).

The vowel Э, э

small	э
capital	Э

This may look backwards to you at first and in Russian is called a 'backwards e'. Unlike the English letter 'e' (which has different sounds depending on the letters around it – think of 'shed' and 'seat'), the Russian э is always pronounced like *e* in l*e*t.

Exercise 4.1

Over to you! Practise saying these Russian words.

Russian	Sound	Meaning
её	ye**yo**	*her, hers*
всё	vsyo	*all, everything*
бут**ы**лка	boot**i**lka	*bottle*
сын	sin (draw the tongue back a bit!)	*son*
эксп**е**рт	eksp**ye**rt	*expert*
экстров**е**рт	ekstrav**ye**rt	*extrovert*

The vowel Ю, ю

This is pronounced like *u* in *u*niversity.

small	ю
capital	Ю

The vowel Я, я

Another letter which might appear to be backwards. This is pronounced like *ya* in *ya*rd.

small	я
capital	Я

Insight

Ы and Я are important in the Russian words for *you*, *we* and *I*:

Я	*I*
ты	*you* (singular and informal – for children, family, friends)
мы	*we*
вы	*you* (plural, and also the polite way to address someone you are meeting for the first time, or a person not well known to you)

Exercise 4.2

Over to you! Practise saying these Russian words.

Russian	Sound	Meaning
юрист	yur**ee**st	*lawyer*
юбка	**yu**bka	*skirt*
Ялта	**Ya**lta	*Yalta*
Италия	Eet**a**leeya	*Italy*

Exercise 4.3

Which of these countries is not in Europe?

	Russian	Sound
1	Испания	Eesp**a**neeya
2	Голландия	Gall**a**ndeeya
3	Япония	Yap**o**neeya
4	Германия	Gyerm**a**neeya
5	Англия	**A**ngleeya

Exercise 4.4

Now try your longest piece of reading so far! The only new word in this sentence is зовут (zav**oo**t), which means *they call*.

Russian	Sound	Meaning
Как её зовут?	Kak ye**yo** zav**oo**t?	*What is she called?* (literally, 'How her they call?')

Now choose the only appropriate name for her from the list in the middle column in order to complete the sentence which means *She is called . . .* :

	Possible names	Sound
Её зову́т _____	Серге́й	Syer**gyeiy**
	Ива́н	Ee**va**n
	Ка́тя	**Ka**tya
	Влади́мир	Vlad**ee**meer
	Бори́с	Bar**ees**

New letters: five consonants

The consonant Ж, ж

This is pronounced like *s* in plea*s*ure. (In transliteration it is usually represented by *zh*.)

small	ж
capital	Ж

The consonant Ц, ц

This is pronounced like *ts* in ra*ts*.

small	ц
capital	Ц

The consonant Ч, ч

This is pronounced like *ch* in *ch*eese.

small	ч
capital	Ч

Insight

The letter Ч occurs in one of the most common words in the Russian language which means *what* or *that*: что. **NB!!** In this very important word, the letter Ч is pronounced 'sh' not 'ch', so the words sounds like 'shto'.

Exercise 4.5

Over to you! Practise saying these Russian words.

Russian	Sound	Meaning
жасми́н	zhasm**ee**n	*jasmine*
жа́рко	zh**a**rka	*hot*
ци́ник	ts**ee**neek	*cynic*
цивилиза́ция	tseeveeleez**a**tseeya	*civilization*
чай	ch**a**iy	*tea*
по́чта	p**o**chta	*post office*

Insight

The word **э́то** means *it/this/that is, they/these/those are*. The phrase **Что э́то?** means *What is this?*, and **Кто э́то?** means *Who is this?*

Что э́то? Э́то омле́т.   *What's that? It's an omelette.*
Кто э́то? Э́то актёры.   *Who are they? They are the actors*

New letters: remaining two consonants

The consonant Ш, ш

This is pronounced like *sh* in *sh*eep.

small	ш
capital	Ш

The consonant Щ, щ

This looks very similar to the previous consonant, but note the extra 'tail'. It is pronounced like *shsh* in 'Engli*sh sh*ampoo'.

small	щ
capital	Щ

Exercise 4.6

Over to you! Practise saying these Russian words.

Russian	Sound	Meaning
шарф	sharf	*scarf*
ша́хматы	sh**a**khmati	*chess*
щи	shshee	*cabbage soup*
ещё	yeshsh**yo**	*still, yet, more*

Exercise 4.7

Here are some leisure activities. Only one is musical – which is it?
Remember to cover up the right-hand column – only look at it if
you are stuck!

	Russian	**Sound**
1	виндсе́рфинг	veends**y**erfeeng
2	джаз	dzhaz
3	пинг-по́нг	peeng-p**o**ng
4	ка́рты	k**a**rti
5	Скрэбл	Skrebl

Signs with no sounds

And finally – two characters which have no sound of their own,
but which affect the way other letters are pronounced.

The 'hard sign' Ъ, ъ

small	ъ
capital	Ъ

The 'soft sign' ъ, ь

small	ь
capital	Ь

Neither of these letters occurs at the
beginning of a word. The hard sign (ъ)
occurs very rarely, is not pronounced and just makes a tiny pause
between syllables:

Russian	Sound	Meaning
отъезд	at **ye**zd	*departure*

The soft sign, which looks very similar (ь), 'softens' the consonant
which precedes it and is especially common after т and л. When
pronouncing the soft sign after the Russian letter т, think of the
way we pronounce the letter *t* in the English word *stew* (as if we're
adding a soft, gentle *y* after the *t*). When pronouncing the Russian
letter л with a soft sign, arch your tongue against your palate (i.e.
not low in the mouth). In transliteration the soft sign is usually
represented as follows:

Russian	Sound	Meaning
мать	mat'	*mother*
чихать	cheekh**a**t'	*to sneeze*

УРА! (oor**a**! *Hurrah!*). We have now met all 33 characters – 11
vowels, 20 consonants and 2 characters (ъ, ь) with no sound of
their own.

Exercise 4.8

Revise the alphabet! Check your knowledge of each letter in the
tables.

Vowel	Sound	Russian	Sound	Meaning
А а	*a* in f*a*ther	банк	bank	*bank*
Е е	*ye* in *ye*t	ресторан	ryestar**a**n	*restaurant*
Ё ё	*yo* in *yo*nder	её	ye**yo**	*her, hers*
И и	*ee* in f*ee*t	вин**о**	veen**o**	*wine*
Й й	*y* in bo*y*	чай	chaiy	*tea*
О о	*o* in bore (when stressed;	**о**фис	**o**fees	office
	otherwise like *a* in sof*a*)	**а**том	**a**tam	*atom*
У у	*oo* in sh*oo*t	суп	soop	*soup*
ы	approximately like *i* in *i*ll	сын	sin	*son*
Э э	*e* in l*e*t	эксп**е**рт	eksp**ye**rt	*expert*
Ю ю	*u* in *u*niversity	юр**и**ст	yur**ee**st	*lawyer*
Я я	*ya* in *ya*rd	Ит**а**лия	Eet**a**leeya	*Italy*

11 vowels done!

Consonant	Sound	Russian	Sound	Meaning
Б б	b in bank	бут**ы**лка	boot**i**lka	bottle
В в	v in visit	в**о**дка	v**o**dka	vodka
Г г	g in goat	гид	geed	guide
Д д	d in daughter	департ**а**мент	dyepart**a**ment	department
Ж ж	s in pleasure	ж**а**рко	zh**a**rka	hot
З з	z in zoo	зуб	zoob	tooth
К к	k in kite	Кан**а**да	Kan**a**da	Canada
Л л	l in lamp	л**а**мпа	l**a**mpa	lamp
М м	m in motor	метр**о**	myetr**o**	metro
Н н	n in novel	н**о**та	n**o**ta	note
П п	p in peach	п**а**спорт	p**a**spart	(music)
Р р	r in rat	р**а**дио	r**a**dee-a	passport
С с	s in sip	сестр**а**	syestr**a**	radio
Т т	t in tired	тр**а**ктор	tr**a**ktar	sister
Ф ф	f in funny	факс	faks	tractor
Х х	ch in loch	хар**а**ктер	khar**a**ktyer	fax
Ц ц	ts in rats	ц**и**ник	ts**ee**neek	character
Ч ч	ch in cheese	чай	chaiy	cynic
Ш ш	sh in sheep	шарф	sharf	tea
Щ щ	shsh in English shampoo	щи	shshee	scarf cabbage soup

20 consonants done!

Sign	Function	Russian word	Sound	Meaning
ъ	Hard sign – makes a tiny pause between syllables	отъ<u>е</u>зд	at **ye**zd	*departure*
ь	Soft sign – adds a soft, gentle 'y' sound after a consonant	мать	mat' (think of how 't' is pronounced in 'stew')	*mother*

Congratulations! Now you have met all the printed characters of the Russian alphabet – the Р<u>У</u>ССКИЙ АЛФАВ<u>И</u>Т (<u>roo</u>skeey alfav<u>ee</u>t).

Insight

Most infinitives (the 'to do' form of the verb) end in a soft sign (ь). Here's a particularly intriguing infinitive which involves борщ (*beetroot soup*): переб<u>о</u>рщить. Literally, this means 'to make too much beetroot soup', but it is used in the sense of 'to go too far, to go over the top'.

ТРЕК (SPORT (

Я Pronounced YA

Е Pronounced YE

Н " N

Ф sound like F in Far

ФАКТ means FACT

Ш is pronounced "sh"

И pronounced ee

В pronounced like V

Р " R like RAT

О like O in bore

Ж like ZH

Ц like TS (TSAr).

COUNTY NATIONAL BANK

CLEARFIELD • KARTHAUS • MADERA • PHILIPSBURG
OSCEOLA MILLS • CHERRY STREET OFFICE AT CLEARFIELD, PA
OLD TOWN ROAD OFFICE AT CLEARFIELD, PA

РОССИЯ (Russia)

ВООРУЖЁННЫЕ
СИЛЫ
s e ya v

voor oo

Ь sounds like
V

Ь р ω phi

Москаа (MOSCOW)

Exercise 4.9

If you were a teetotaller, which of the following drinks would you order? The right-hand column is for emergencies only!

1	вин<u>о</u>	veen<u>o</u>
2	в<u>и</u>ски	v<u>ee</u>skee
3	в<u>о</u>дка	v<u>o</u>dka
4	лимон<u>а</u>д	leeman<u>a</u>d
5	шамп<u>а</u>нское	shamp<u>a</u>nskaye

Names

We have already met a range of common Russian first names. Now we are going to look at surnames and what are known as 'patronymics'. The patronymic is a middle name created from the father's first name. The most polite form of address is to use someone's first name, followed by their patronymic (for example, you would address your teacher or your boss by their first name and patronymic). If you are a man, add **-ович** to your father's first name if it ends in a consonant, or **-евич** if it ends in **-й** (removing the **й** first).

First name	Patronymic	Surname	
Бор<u>и</u>с	Никол<u>а</u>евич	Помог<u>а</u>ев	is the father of →
Серг<u>е</u>й	Бор<u>и</u>сович	Помог<u>а</u>ев	is the father of →
Ив<u>а</u>н	Серг<u>е</u>евич	Помог<u>а</u>ев	

If you are a woman, add **-овна** to your father's first name if it ends in a consonant, or **-евна** if it ends in **й** (removing the **й** first).

First name	Patronymic	Surname	
Борис	Николаевич	Помогаев	is the father of →
Татьяна	Борисовна	Помогаева	
Николай	Владимирович	Помогаев	is the father of →
Надежда	Николаевна	Помогаева	

Note that a woman's surname usually ends in -а or -ая, whereas a man's surname usually ends in a consonant or -ский.

Exercise 4.10

Look at the full names (surname – фамилия, patronymic – отчество and first name – имя) of the following two people:

1 фамилия: Кузнецова
   отчество: Валентиновна
   имя: Анна

2 фамилия: Горбунов
   отчество: Викторович
   имя: Андрей

1 What is the first name of Anna's father?
2 What is the first name of Andrei's father?

Exercise 4.11

Meet the Bykov family! First look at the Russian words for the members of the various generations.

Russian	Sound	Meaning
б**а**бушка	b**a**booshka	*grandmother*
д**е**душка	d**ye**dooshka	*grandfather*
мать (м**а**ма)	mat' (m**a**ma)	*mother (mummy)*
от**е**ц (п**а**па)	at**ye**ts (p**a**pa)	*father (daddy)*
сын	sin	*son*
дочь	doch'	*daughter*
д**я**дя	d**ya**dya	*uncle*
т**ё**тя	t**yo**tya	*aunt*
внук	vnook	*grandson*
вн**у**чка	vn**oo**chka	*granddaughter*

Now look at the family tree below:

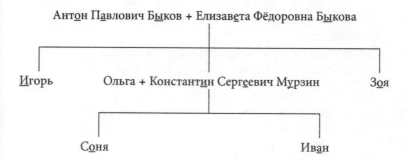

Ант**о**н П**а**влович Б**ы**ков + Елизав**е**та Фёдоровна Б**ы**кова

Иг**о**рь   Ольга + Констант**и**н Серг**е**евич М**у**рзин   З**о**я

С**о**ня   Ив**а**н

Now answer the following questions.

1 What relation is Ив**а**н Констант**и**нович М**у**рзин to Ант**о**н
П**а**влович Б**ы**ков?
2 Two people will have the patronymic Ант**о**новна. What are their
first names?
3 What is the patronymic of С**о**ня?

Exercise 4.12

Look carefully at this advertisement for a concert and find the information to answer the following questions (a translation of the advertisement is given in the Key).

1 In which month is the concert taking place?
2 Which two composers are featured?
3 What is the name of the pianist?

Театр оперы и балета
КОНЦЕРТ
30 октября (в 12 часов)

Паганини
Концерт номер 1 для скрипки с оркестром
солист Александр Чирков
Рахманинов
Концерт номер 2 для фортепьяно с оркестром
солист Николай Байков

Exercise 4.13

All but one of the ten words in the table are connected with the world of finance. Find the odd one out (remember to cover up the right-hand column!).

Russian	Sound
банк	bank
кредит	kryed**ee**t
кредитная карточка	kryed**ee**tnaya k**a**rtachka
инвестиция	eenvyest**ee**tseeya
финансовый кризис	feen**a**nsaviy kr**ee**zees

космон**а**вт	kasman**a**vt
д**о**ллары	d**o**llari
экон**о**мика	ekan**o**meeka
капит**а**л	kapeet**a**l
банк**и**р	bank**ee**r

....

Check that you've understood the meaning of all the words by looking in the Key.

End-of-unit review – things to remember, tips and questions

(Answers to the questions are in the Key.)

1 Remember that что (*what, that, which*) is pronounced 'shto'.

2 Two key questions based on это are: Что это? *What is it/this/ that? What are they/these/those?*, and Кто это? *Who is it/this/ that? Who are they/these/those?*

3 There are two words for *you*: ты is the word to use for a child, member of the family or friend, and вы is for plural use, or singular for someone you do not know well or are meeting for the first time.

4 The hard sign and the soft sign have no sound of their own; both affect the sound of other letters. The hard sign is very rare, but the soft sign is very common.

5 A patronymic is the middle name based on the father's first name, and the most polite form of address is to use someone's first name followed by his/her patronymic.

6 In this unit you met the two most famous kinds of Russian soup: борщ (*beetroot soup*) and щи (*cabbage soup*).

7 Something beginning with P: can you work out what the following three words mean in English?

риск, ритуал, рутина

8 Something beginning with C: can you work out what the following three words mean in English?

сервер, скандал, сноб

9 Something beginning with T: can you work out what the following three words mean in English?

телеканал, тест, трофей

10 Something beginning with Ф: can you work out what the following three words mean in English?

финал, фокус-группа, формула

5

....

Revision and reading practice

In this unit you will
- **Learn the proper order of the letters in the Cyrillic alphabet**
- **Have lots of practice in reading words**
- **Learn about months of the year and days of the week in Russian**

The aim of this unit is to help you to consolidate your knowledge of the printed alphabet. In Unit 5 you'll have more practice in reading words and short phrases, but transliteration will not be given in Units 5–10. Learning the proper order of the alphabet is essential for later study if you need to use a dictionary or vocabulary list.

Remember that Russian has no present tense of the verb to be (*I am*, *you are*, etc.), so it's very easy to make statements in the present tense. Look at the following examples and note that when making statements of this kind, a dash is often inserted (almost as if you were using the sign =):

Борис—инженер.	*Boris is an engineer.*
Светлана—медсестра.	*Svetlana is a nurse.* (literally, a 'medical sister')
Игорь—журналист.	*Igor is a journalist.*

Exercise 5.1

Look at the pictures opposite and decide which of the professions below fit which picture.

1

2

3

4

Insight

The words in 5.1 are all nouns (words which name someone or something). Russian has three 'genders' (groups) of nouns: masculine, feminine and neuter. The last letter usually shows us the gender of the noun:

Last letter: consonant, -ь, -й   = masculine
                  -а , -я, -ь   = feminine
                  -о, -е   = neuter

Exercise 5.2

Look at the words a–h in the list above in Exercise 5.1. Did you understand them all? Check their meanings in the Key.

Asking questions is just as easy as making statements if you know the key question words. Here are four important ones:

где?	where?
как?	how?
когда?	when?
кто?	who?

And examples of how we use them in questions:

Где Борис?	Where is Boris?
Как её зовут?	What is she called? (literally 'how her they call?')
Кто Светлана?	Who is Svetlana? (This is also the Russian way of saying: What does Svetlana do (as a job)?
Когда матч?	When is the match?

Exercise 5.3

You can answer the questions about Boris, Svetlana and the match by reading the following sentences. Complete the English answers that follow them:

Борис в супермаркете.
Светлана – актриса.
Матч в 21 час.

1 Boris is in the _____ .
2 Svetlana is an _____ .
3 The match is at _____ o'clock.

Correction

As well as making statements and asking questions, remember that you can also easily contradict statements by using **не**. Look at the following examples – some words are in brackets to remind you that the present tense of the verb *to be* and articles (the/a) do not exist in Russian:

Нет! Борис не теннисист, он боксёр.	*No! Boris (is) not (a) tennis player – he (is a) boxer.*
Нет! Она не медсестра, она физиотерапевт.	*No! she (is) not (a) nurse – she (is a) physiotherapist.*
Нет! Чайковский не космонавт, он композитор.	*No! Tchaikovsky (is) not (an) astronaut – he (is a) composer.*

Exercise 5.4

Look at the examples above once more and then answer these questions:

1 What is the Russian word for *he*?
2 What is the Russian word for *she*?

Insight

О**н** means *he* or *it* (for masculine nouns).

Он**а** means *she* or *it* (for feminine nouns).

Он**о** means *it* (for neuter nouns).

Он**и** means *they* (for all plural nouns).

Где те**а**тр? – Вот он. *Where's the theatre? There it is.*

Где м**е**сто? – Вот он**о**. *Where's the seat? There it is.*

Exercise 5.5

Look at the pictures below and then at the following statements, which are incorrect. Complete the corrected versions which follow.

1 В**и**ктор – журнал**и**ст.

2 Вад**и**м – жок**е**й.

3 Алекс**а**ндр – гимн**а**ст.

1 Нет! В**и**ктор не журнал**и**ст, он _____ .

2 Нет! Вад**и**м не жок**е**й, он _____ .

3 Нет! Алекс**а**ндр не гимн**а**ст, он _____ .

1 Ви**ктор**

2 Вади**м**

3 Алекса**ндр**

Vocabulary

Most of the words we have met so far have been 'cognates', i.e. they sound very much like their English counterparts (see list A below). Of course, not all Russian words follow this pattern; although there are many which have a familiar sound, there are some which are more closely linked with Greek, Latin or with another modern European language (see list B), and others which sound nothing like their equivalents in English (see list C). Now look at the three lists of words. They are all connected with university life. You should find list A the easiest!

A

профе́ссор	*professor*
семина́р	*seminar*
студе́нт	*student*
университе́т	*university*

B

библиоте́ка	*library*
ка́федра	*university department*

C

иссле́дование	*research*
преподава́тель	*lecturer*

Exercise 5.6

Months of the year fall more or less into the 'A' group, i.e. their sound is recognizably similar to their English counterparts. Look at the months in the following list. Can you put them into calendar order? January has been done for you!

a май

b октя́брь

c февра́ль

d ию́нь

e дека́брь

f янва́рь = 1

g	июль	**j**	сент<u>я</u>брь
h	март	**k**	<u>а</u>вгуст
i	но<u>я</u>брь	**l**	апр<u>е</u>ль

Days of the week, in total contrast, have very little connection with their English counterparts (although speakers of Italian and Spanish will recognize the word for *Saturday*):

Дни недели *Days of the week*

Russian word	Meaning	Derivation
понед<u>е</u>льник	*Monday*	*the Russian word for 'week'*
вт<u>о</u>рник	*Tuesday*	*the Russian word for 'second'*
ср<u>е</u>да	*Wednesday*	*the Russian word for 'middle'*
четв<u>е</u>рг	*Thursday*	*the Russian word for 'four'*
п<u>я</u>тница	*Friday*	*the Russian word for 'five'*
субб<u>о</u>та	*Saturday*	*the word 'sabbath'*
воскрес<u>е</u>нье	*Sunday*	*the Russian word for 'resurrection'*

Exercise 5.7

Vladimir is a television addict who likes to plan his week's viewing in advance. Look at the list he has made, then answer the questions that follow:

Понедельник	10.10	Телесериал: Солдаты
Вторник	20.55	Кинофильм: Авиакатастрофа
Среда	21.35	Документальный фильм: Легенды театра
Четверг	12.55	Ток-шоу: Клуб футболистов
Пятница	15.45	Чемпионат: формула-1
Суббота	24.00	Гороскоп
Воскресенье	21.00	Комедия: Астерикс и Обеликс: Миссия Клеопатра

On what day does Vladimir plan to watch:

1 a talk show?
2 motor racing?
3 a film about a plane crash?
4 a comedy?
5 a serial about soldiers?
6 a documentary film?
7 a horoscope programme?

Insight

You will have noticed that a lot of the television vocabulary in 5.7 is based on English words. This is also true of the vocabulary relating to books. Here is a list of examples in alphabetical order:

бестселлер	*best seller*
детектив	*detective story*
хеппи-энд	*happy ending*

Time to put all the characters we have learnt into alphabetical order. You have already met all the words given as examples, except:

| Европа | Europe |
| ёж | hedgehog |

А а	is for адрес
Б б	is for банк
В в	is for водка
Г г	is for гид
Д д	is for департамент
Е е	is for Европа
Ё ё	is for ёж
Ж ж	is for журналист
З з	is for зоопарк
И и	is for инженер
Й й	is for Йорк
К к	is for клуб
Л л	is for лимонад
М м	is for матч
Н н	is for ноябрь
О о	is for офис
П п	is for паспорт
Р р	is for радио
С с	is for суп
Т т	is for такси
У у	is for университет
Ф ф	is for факс
Х х	is for хоккеист
Ц ц	is for цивилизация
Ч ч	is for чай
Ш ш	is for шампанское
Щ щ	is for щи
ъ	No sound of its own and never used as the first letter of a word. See Unit 4.
ы	Never used as the first letter of a word. For pronunciation, see Unit 4.
ь	No sound of its own and never used as the first letter of a word. See Unit 4.
Э э	is for эксперт
Ю ю	is for юрист
Я я	is for Ялта

Insight

Another picturesque Russian phrase! – the word **ёж** (hedgehog) features in a phrase which literally means *it is understandable even to a hedgehog* and which is the Russian equivalent of *any fool could tell* or *it's as plain as day*: **и** (*and/even*) **ежу** (*to a hedgehog*) **понятно** (*it is understandable/clear*).

Exercise 5.8

You are a tour guide and need to make an alphabetical list of the members of your group. Number 1 is indicated for you.

List of surnames	Position in alphabet
Кондратов	
Селезнев	
Носиков	
Бармина	1
Хоботова	
Лев	
Грязнова	
Вереев	
Туманова	
Давыдов	

How many members of the group are women?

Exercise 5.9

You are in charge of the small ads section in a newspaper office. Put the following advertisement sections into alphabetical order.

ТАЙМШЕР
КОМПЬЮТЕРЫ
АВТОЦЕНТР
БИЗНЕС
ТЕЛЕВИЗОРЫ
АНТИКВАРИАТ

Which section relates to:

1 cars?
2 antiques?
3 time share?
4 computers?
5 business?

Exercise 5.10

When you're looking at words which don't sound like their English equivalent, it's important to be able to find them in a dictionary or vocabulary list. Masha has made a list of the presents she intends to buy for birthdays this year. She is a very organized person and has put the names of her friends and family in alphabetical order on the left. Using the vocabulary list to help you, answer the questions that follow:

Vocabulary list

велосип<u>ед</u>	*bicycle*
дух<u>и</u>	*perfume*
кн<u>и</u>га по футб<u>о</u>лу	*book on football*
конф<u>е</u>ты	*sweets*
ч<u>а</u>йник	*teapot*
кулин<u>а</u>рная кн<u>и</u>га	*cookery book*

| мишка | *teddy bear* |
| платье | *dress* |

Masha's list

Анна	←	духи
Бабушка	←	чайник
Вадим	←	велосипед
Валентин	←	мишка
Дедушка	←	конфеты
Константин	←	книга по футболу
Максим	←	кулинарная книга
Соня	←	платье

Who is going to receive:

1 a dress?
2 perfume?
3 a cookery book?
4 sweets?
5 a teapot?

Exercise 5.11

Look at the theatre ticket and use the vocabulary list to help you answer the questions which follow. (NB You do not need to understand all the words on the ticket in order to answer the questions!)

Vocabulary list

имени	*named after*
место	*place, seat*
начало спектаклей	*beginning of performances*
партер	*stalls*
Пермский	*belonging to Perm* (a city in the Urals)
правая сторона	*right-hand side*
ряд	*row*
цена	*price*

1 After which composer is the theatre named?

Пермский государственный театр оперы и балета
имени А. П. Чайковского

ПАРТЕР
Правая сторона   **Ряд 5 Место 9**

Спектакль начинается в 19 часов 30 минут
Дети до 16 лет на вечерние спектакли не допускаются

---

2 In which row will you be sitting?
3 When do performances begin?

Exercise 5.12

Which of the following words is not a subject which might be
studied at school?

география
химия
формула-1
математика
история
музыка

If you were to put this list of words into alphabetical order, which
would come first and which would come last?

Insight

Some Russian words are recognizable even though they don't resemble their English counterparts exactly, e.g. математика means *mathematics*, and геометрия means *geometry*. Remember that saying words out loud can help you to recognize their meaning. Here (in alphabetical order!) are some more mathematical words:

алгебра	*algebra*
минус	*minus*
плюс	*plus*
фракция	*fraction*

End-of-unit review – things to remember, tips and questions

(Answers to the questions are in the Key.)

1 There are three groups ('genders') of nouns in Russian: masculine, feminine and neuter. You can recognize which group a noun belongs to by looking at its last letter.

2 The only ending shared by masculine and feminine nouns is the soft sign, so whenever you meet a soft sign noun for the first time, be sure to learn whether it is masculine or feminine.

3 All the months of the year are masculine (and many end in a soft sign).

4 The word имени is often found in the names of buildings (academies, galleries, libraries, theatres, universities, etc.) which are named after famous people. Literally, имени means *of the name of*.

5 Чай means *tea*, which is a very important part of Russian culture; ча́йник is a *kettle* or *teapot*. (Colloquially, ча́йник also means a *novice* or *inexperienced person*.)

6 Three important question words beginning with K: как? *how?* когда *when?* кто *who?*

7 Something beginning with Д: can you work out what the following three words mean in English?

демонстра́ция, дие́та, диза́йнер

8 Something beginning with И: can you work out what the following three words mean in English?

иде́я, изоля́ция, инспе́ктор

9 Something beginning with Ц: can you work out what the following three words mean in English?

цеме́нт, центр, цикл

10 Put the following words in alphabetical order and work out their meanings:

ю́мор, нерв, субъе́кт, стресс, ноутбу́к, органи́зм

6

The cursive script (1)

In this unit you will
- *Meet the handwritten (or 'cursive') form of the first 16 letters of the alphabet*
- *Learn more about Russian names*
- *Learn some useful words for tourists visiting a Russian city*

It is very useful to be able to recognize the handwritten script as it is often used for decorative effect in advertisements, on greetings cards, theatre programmes and so on, as well as in handwritten letters, notes, etc. With one or two exceptions, the handwritten characters are not too strikingly different from their printed equivalents. Note that Russians would never write in the stress marks, so we haven't.

Handwritten characters

Here are the first 16 handwritten characters: compare them with their printed equivalents:

Printed capital	Handwritten capital	Printed small	Handwritten small
А	*А*	а	*а*
Б	*Б*	б	*б*
В	*В*	в	*в*

Printed capital	Handwritten capital	Printed small	Handwritten small
Г	*Г*	г	*г*
Д	*Д*	д	*д ∂*
Е	*Е*	е	*е*
Ё	*Ё*	ё	*ё*
Ж	*Ж*	ж	*ж*
З	*З*	з	*з*
И	*И*	и	*и*
Й	*Й*	й	*й*
К	*К*	к	*к*
Л	*Л*	л	*л*
М	*М*	м	*м*
Н	*Н*	н	*н*
О	*О*	о	*о*

Some of these need more getting used to than others.

The small version of г may look 'backwards' to you at first – it might help you to think of it as a backwards 's'.

Notice that there are two ways of handwriting the small letter д.

Full words

The real fun starts when full words are written. Notice particularly:

л *л*

м *м*

These must always begin with a little hook, so they are clear in combination with other letters.

Exercise 6.1

Practise your recognition of the first 16 handwritten letters: cover up the first (printed) column until you have tried to read the handwritten words. If you want to practise writing yourself, try writing the word in the third column and compare your results with the second column!

Printed word	Handwritten word	Your version	Meaning
<u>А</u>виа	*Авиа*		Airmail
Бан<u>а</u>н	*Банан*		Banana
Вин<u>о</u>	*Вино*		Wine
Гол	*Гол*		Goal
Да	*Да*		Yes
Ед<u>а</u>	*Еда*		Food
Ёлка	*Ёлка*		Fir tree
Жен<u>а</u>	*Жена*		Wife
З<u>о</u>на	*Зона*		Zone
Ид<u>е</u>ал	*Идеал*		Ideal
Й<u>о</u>га	*Йога*		Yoga
Кин<u>о</u>	*Кино*		Cinema
Лим<u>о</u>н	*Лимон*		Lemon
Молок<u>о</u>	*Молоко*		Milk
Не	*Нет*		No
Од<u>е</u>жда	*Одежда*		Clothes

Exercise 6.2

Which is the odd one out in the following list? Cover up the right-hand column unless you're really stuck.

Handwritten	Printed
1 *вино*	в<u>и</u>но
2 *водка*	в<u>о</u>дка
3 *лимонад*	лимон<u>а</u>д
4 *май*	май
5 *молоко*	молок<u>о</u>

Exercise 6.3

Party time! Boris is making a list of friends to invite to his party. Match the handwritten Russian versions on the left with the English versions on the right.

1 *Елена*	**a** Ivan
2 *Вадим*	**b** Anna
3 *Иван*	**c** Elena
4 *Анна*	**d** Evgeny
5 *Евгений*	**e** Vadim

Diminutives

All the first names above are the 'full' form. Russian makes considerable use of diminutive forms of first names, as an indication of closeness, affection or endearment. Here are some common Russian first names and their affectionate diminutive forms:

Full		Diminutive
Андр<u>е</u>й	→	Андр<u>ю</u>ша
<u>А</u>нна	→	<u>А</u>ня, <u>А</u>ничка
Бор<u>и</u>с	→	Б<u>о</u>ря
Влад<u>и</u>мир	→	Вол<u>о</u>дя, В<u>о</u>ва
Ел<u>е</u>на	→	Л<u>е</u>на, Л<u>е</u>ночка
Ир<u>и</u>на	→	<u>И</u>ра, <u>И</u>рочка

Константин	→	Костя
Николай	→	Коля
Ольга	→	Оля, Оленька

These diminutive forms are used to address close friends, family and small children. The polite, formal way to address people is to use their first name and their patronymic, so if your boss is called Константин Николаевич Зеленов, you will address him as Константин Николаевич. If your son is called Константин, you would probably address him as Костя (unless you're very cross with him!).

Insight

Luckily, most diminutive forms of first names bear a close resemblance to the original; it is trickier if the diminutive starts with a different letter:

| Александр | → | Саша |
| Елена | → | Лена |

To practise reading the alphabet, try this range of diminutive forms of the name Мария:

Маша
Маруся
Маня
Манюня

Exercise 6.4

More famous names! Who is the odd one out in this list of five famous Russians?

1 Чехов
2 Толстой

3 Достоевский
4 Рахманинов
5 Пушкин

Famous Russians

The famous five include four of Russia's greatest writers and one composer. Practise reading their names in full. We start with the writer who was Russia's first truly great poet.

Name	Dates	One famous work
Александр Сергеевич Пушкин	1799–1837	Евгений Онегин (novel in verse – *Eugene Onegin*)
Фёдор Михайлович Достоевский	1821–81	Братья Карамазовы (novel – *The Brothers Karamazov*)
Лев Николаевич Толстой	1828–1910	Война и мир (novel – *War and Peace*)
Антон Павлович Чехов	1860–1904	Дядя Ваня (play – *Uncle Vanya*)
Сергей Васильевич Рахманинов	1873–1943	Концерт номер 2 для фортепьяно с оркестром (Concerto no. 2 for Piano and Orchestra)

Insight

Russian grammar has a system of 'case endings' (as in Latin and German, for example); the different case endings on Russian words alter their meanings. At this stage of learning the alphabet, you can still work out meanings of short phrases without knowing the cases.

Exercise 6.5

Look at the two extracts from advertisements and then answer the questions in English. (Look at the questions first!).

1 Which advertisement is from an estate agent and which from a travel agent?
2 What three buildings is the estate agent selling? What is claimed about the quality of these buildings?
3 Which countries are advertised by the travel agent? What activities are on offer in these countries?

Advertisement A

ТУРИНФО
АВСТРАЛИЯ –
виндсерфинг
серфинг
АВСТРИЯ –
автобусные туры
АФРИКА
сафари в национальных
парках

Advertisement B

АГЕНТСТВО-А1
ОФИС
ФИТНЕС-ЦЕНТР
ПАРКИНГ НА 50
АВТОМОБИЛЕЙ
класс А!!!!!

Insight

Дом is the Russian word for *house* or *home*. If you add the letter 'a' to it, you get the expression for *at home*: до́ма.

Дом has other meanings too, for example:

| многоэта́жный дом | *block of flats* (literally, *multi-storey house*) |
| дом Рома́новых | *the House of Romanov* |

Vocabulary

If you are staying in Russia as a tourist or on business, there are a number of key words you will need to recognize. Some sound familiar.

ви́за	visa
гид	guide
па́спорт	passport
тури́зм	tourism
тури́ст	tourist
экску́рсия	excursion

Some key words are a little less obvious, although once you know their derivation they're easy to remember:

- When you arrive at your hotel you might be asked to fill in a **бланк** (*form* – which is, of course, blank until you fill it in).
- If you stay in a hotel you are a guest – hence the word for *hotel* **гости́ница**, which comes from the Russian **гость** (*guest*).
- In a hotel your room will have a number – hence the word for *hotel room*, **но́мер**, clearly a close relation of the English word *number*.

Exercise 6.6

Armed with the information just given, can you complete the кроссво́рд (overleaf)?

ПО ГОРИЗОНТА́ЛИ (Across)
1 Person who shows tourists round museum
2 You need this to enter other countries and return to your own

ПО ВЕРТИКА́ЛИ (Down)
1 A place where tourists stay
2 You might go here to see a play, opera or ballet

ПО ГОРИЗОНТАЛИ (Across)   ПО ВЕРТИКАЛИ (Down)

3 You need one of these documents in order to enter Russia

4 You need to buy one of these if you want to travel by train, plane or bus

5 Your hotel room

		¹		Д		
		О				
²			П			Т
	³					
	⁴	И			²	
					е	
	⁵	О				

Insight

Russians are noted for their hospitality, so it seems a little unfair that the Russian equivalent of *there's no place like home* literally means 'as a guest it's good, but at home it's better':

В гостях (*as a guest*) **хорошо** (*it's good*), **а** (*but*) **дома** (*at home*) **лучше** (*it's better*).

Vocabulary

When in Russia, it's important to understand the signs that tell you what's where.

банк	*bank*
вход	*entrance*
вы́ход	*exit*
перехо́д	*crossing* (or *subway*)
по́чта	*post office*
ста́нция метро́	*metro station*
у́лица	*street*

Be prepared for the endings of words to vary. Take care if you see this sign.

НЕТ ВХОДА!

Don't go in! The key here is нет (*no*).

Insight

Вы́ход means *exit* because the prefix (letters added to the beginning of a word) ВЫ- means *out of*, and they have been added to ход, which indicates movement on foot. The prefix В- means *into*, which is why вход means entrance.

Exercise 6.7

In the left-hand column are some words you may come across in a Russian city. Match them up with their meanings in the right-hand column.

1 ка́сса   **a** taxi rank
2 кио́ск   **b** ticket office, cash desk

3 медпункт	c centre
4 милиция	d kiosk
5 остановка автобуса	e telephone box
6 стоянка такси	f bus stop
7 телефон автомат	g police
8 центр	h first aid

Currency

As a visitor to Russia you will also need to look out for this sign:

ОБМЕН ВАЛЮТЫ

This tells you where you can cash in your traveller's cheques or change money (in English, *foreign currency exchange*.)

Notice how close the second of these words, **ВАЛЮТА** (*foreign currency*), is in sound to the English word *value*.

Exercise 6.8

Look at the list of foreign countries below. Can you work out what they are in English?

1 Норвегия
2 Италия
3 Канада
4 Англия
5 Финляндия
6 Голландия
7 Украина
8 Австрия
9 Франция
10 Австралия

If you are a tourist travelling from a foreign country to Russia, you will need to change your money into roubles (рубли), so you'll be interested to find out about the exchange rate: валютный курс.

Exercise 6.9

You have just arrived at your hotel in Moscow and are checking through the information leaflet in your room. Most of the words used are 'cognates' (sound roughly like their English equivalents), but there are three which aren't:

врач *doctor*   услуги *service*   этаж *storey, floor*

Look at the information and answer the questions which follow.

АВИАБИЛЕТЫ	☎ 2549
БАНК	
1 этаж	
БАРЫ	☎ 2050
1, 2, 15 этажи	
БИЗНЕС-ЦЕНТР (факс,	
Электронная почта, Интернет)	☎ 2688
1 этаж	
БИЛЬЯРДНАЯ	☎ 2692
БУФЕТ	☎ 2031
1, 3, 5, 7, 9, 14 этажи	
ВРАЧ	☎ 2416
2 этаж	
ПОЧТА	
1 этаж	
САУНА	☎ 2488
СЕЙФЫ	☎ 2458
СУВЕНИРЫ, Сувенирный киоск,	
2 этаж	
ТАКСИ	☎ 2091
ТЕАТРАЛЬНЫЕ БИЛЕТЫ	☎ 2027
ЭКСКУРСИИ	☎ 2027

Which number would you ring if you wanted to:

1 Visit the sauna?
2 Enquire about plane tickets?
3 Book tickets for the theatre?

Which floor would you need to go to if you wanted to:

4 See the doctor?
5 Buy some souvenirs?
6 Send a fax?

Buildings

In Russian hotels, the ground floor is the first floor (so the English first floor in Russia is 2 эта́ж).

Exercise 6.10

The following list contains the sorts of books that are best sellers. The list shows their order of popularity (their ре́йтинг).

Бестсе́ллеры	Ре́йтинг
	1 Детекти́в
	2 Автобиогра́фия
	3 Ю́мор
	4 Биогра́фия
	5 Истори́ческий романти́зм

1 What five categories of book are listed?
2 Now put the five categories in alphabetical order.

End-of-unit review – things to remember, tips and questions

(Answers to the questions are in the Key.)

1 The small handwritten letter г looks like the letter *s* backwards.

2 Эт<u>а</u>ж means *floor, storey*. 1 эт<u>а</u>ж (п<u>е</u>рвый эт<u>а</u>ж) means *ground floor*.

3 Most names of countries end in -ия (and are therefore feminine), but note this small selection of places which do not fit the -ия model: Ам<u>е</u>рика (*America*), <u>А</u>фрика (*Africa*), Изр<u>а</u>иль (*Israel*), Кан<u>а</u>да (*Canada*) and Кит<u>а</u>й (*China*). (Note that Изр<u>а</u>иль ends in a soft sign, so we need to check the gender – it is a masculine word.)

4 When М and Л are handwritten, they must start with a small hook.

5 Н<u>о</u>мер can mean *hotel room* as well as *number* (e.g. н<u>о</u>мер телеф<u>о</u>на).

6 Гост<u>и</u>ница means *hotel;* you will also come across the word от<u>е</u>ль with the same meaning (and it's a masculine word).

7 If you wanted to see a doctor, which of the following signs would you follow?

врач   бар   с<u>а</u>уна

8 If you wanted to post some cards, which of the following signs would you follow?

сейфы,   почта,   бильярдная

9 If you wanted to leave a building, which of these two signs would you follow: вход or выход?

10 Put the following words in alphabetical order:

это,   элегантный,   экзамен,   экскурсия,   эксперт

7

The cursive script (2)

In this unit you will
- **Learn how to recognize the whole of the Cyrillic alphabet in cursive form**
- **Learn about greetings**
- **Learn about seasons and weather in Russia**

Handwritten characters

Here are the last 15 handwritten characters (and two signs).
Compare them with their printed equivalents:

Printed capital	Handwritten capital	Printed small	Handwritten small
П	*Π*	п	*n*
Р	*Р*	р	*р*
С	*С*	с	*с*
Т	*ЛГ*	т	*m, т*
У	*У*	у	*У*
Ф	*Ф*	ф	*ф*
Х	*Х*	х	*х*

Printed capital	Handwritten capital	Printed small	Handwritten small
Ц	*Ц*	ц	*ц*
Ч	*Ч*	ч	*ч*
Ш	*Ш*	ш	*ш*
Щ	*Щ*	щ	*щ*
		ъ	*ъ*
		ы	*ы*
		ь	*ь*
Э	*Э*	э	*э*
Ю	*Ю*	ю	*ю*
Я	*Я*	я	*я*

Notice that there are two ways of handwriting the small letter т. When it is written as *т* it is sometimes written with a line above it (*т̄*). Similarly, a line can be used below the letter *ш* (*ш̱*). This makes them easier to distinguish from the letters they are joined on to.

Like the letters л and м, the letter *я* must always begin with a little hook, so it is clear in combination with other letters.

Exercise 7.1

Practise your recognition of the last batch of handwritten letters: cover up the first (printed) column until you have tried to read the first handwritten word. If you want to practise writing yourself, try writing the word in the third column and compare your results with the second column.

Printed word	Handwritten word	Your version	Meaning
По́чта	*Почта*		Post office
Рестора́н	*Ресторан*		Restaurant
Студе́нт	*Студент*		Student
Тури́ст	*Турист*		Tourist
Университе́т	*Университет*		University
Футбо́л	*Футбол*		Football
Хокке́й	*Хоккей*		Hockey
Центр	*Центр*		Centre
Чай	*Чай*		Tea
Ша́хматы	*Шахматы*		Chess
Щи	*Щи*		Cabbage soup
Отъе́зд*	*Отъезд*		Departure
Вы*	*Вы*		You (polite form)
То́лько*	*Только*		Only
Эта́ж	*Этаж*		Storey, Floor
Ю́бка	*Юбка*		Skirt
Язы́к	*Язык*		Language, Tongue

*The letters ъ, ы, ь are never found at the beginning of a word.

Exercise 7.2

Which is the odd one out in the following list? Cover up the right-hand column unless you're really stuck.

Handwritten	Printed
1 *актёр*	актёр
2 *балет*	бал<u>е</u>т
3 *опера*	<u>о</u>пера
4 *театр*	те<u>а</u>тр
5 *шахматы*	ш<u>а</u>хматы

Insight

Adjectives are words which describe nouns. Adjectives which describe masculine nouns often end in -ный. If the beginning of the adjective is based on a cognate, it shouldn't be too difficult to work out what it means. For example:

музык<u>а</u>льный инструм<u>е</u>нт	*musical instrument*
театр<u>а</u>льный сез<u>о</u>н	*theatre season*

To greet someone informally (*Hi!*) in Russian, say **Прив<u>е</u>т!** (literally, *greetings!*); an informal way to say 'goodbye' is **Пок<u>а</u>!** (*Bye! See you!*). The more formal way of saying 'hello' to someone you would call вы, or to more than one person, is to say **Здр<u>а</u>вствуйте!** (literally, *Be healthy*); if you are talking to someone you call ты, then you would say **Здр<u>а</u>вствуй!** The formal way to say 'goodbye' literally means *until the meeting* (i.e. *until we meet again* – a bit like *au revoir* in French): **До свид<u>а</u>ния!** (this is pronounced as one word, so the 'o' in **до** sounds like the 'a' in *sofa*). If you know you are going to see someone tomorrow, then you can say *until tomorrow*: **До з<u>а</u>втра!** (again, pronounced as one word, so the 'o' in **до** sounds like the 'a' in *sofa*. If you're meeting someone for the first time and want to say *pleased to meet you,* say **<u>О</u>чень при<u>я</u>тно!** (literally, 'it is very pleasant').

Exercise 7.3

Fill in the missing letters of the greetings on the left (the meanings are on the right to help you).

1. п_ка — *bye*
2. до завт_а — *see you tomorrow*
3. _дравствуйте — *hello*
4. очень прият_о — *pleased to meet you*
5. пр_вет — *hi*

Greetings cards are a popular way of celebrating festivals, just as they are in England. The most common greeting you will see on a card is one which will cover all occasions:

С праздником!   *Best wishes* (literally, 'with the celebration')

Other popular ones include:

С днём рождения   *Happy Birthday!* (literally, 'with day of birth')

С Новым годом!   *Happy New Year!* (literally, 'with the new year')

Счастья в Новом году!   *Happiness in the New Year!*

There are greetings cards, too, for Christmas (Orthodox Christmas is celebrated on January 7) and Easter. The greeting you are likely to see on a Christmas card is:

С Рождеством!   (literally, 'with Christmas')

or

С Рождеством Христовым!   (literally, 'with the Nativity of Christ'. 'Nativity' means 'the occasion of a person's birth', which is why the expression for 'Happy Birthday' sounds a little bit similar.)

Easter cards are usually a bit more complex and include part or all of the Orthodox Easter greeting:

Христос воскресе!   *Christ is risen!*
Воистину воскресе!   *Christ is risen indeed!*

Now you can see very clearly where the Russian for 'Sunday' (воскресенье) has come from.

С днём рождения *Happy Birthday!*

Exercise 7.4

On special occasions you might want to give flowers as a present. What are the flowers in the list below? There is a missing letter in each word – can you work out what it is?

1 на_цисс   daffodil (narcissus)
2 глади_лус   gladiolus
3 хри_антёма   chrysanthemum
4 примул_   primula

The missing letters spell the name of another flower. What is it? _ _ _ _

> ## Insight
> Цветы (*flowers*) are a good present to give if you receive an invitation to a Russian home. Make sure you take an <u>uneven</u> number (an even number is associated with funerals), and avoid yellow (жёлтый) flowers, which are traditionally considered unlucky.

Exercise 7.5

Or you might want to give a useful book! Look at the advertisement below in which the company Мир русской культуры (The World of Russian Culture) is advertising five new encyclopaedias.

What are the topics of these five encyclopaedias?

НОВАЯ СЕРИЯ!!

Популярная медицинская энциклопедия

Энциклопедия русской истории

Энциклопедия русской литературы

Энциклопедия русской музыки

Энциклопедия скандалов

Exercise 7.6

In Unit 5 we looked at months of the year. Six months of the year appear in the right-hand column. Select the appropriate month to match the occasions on the left:

1	Christmas in Russia	**a**	октя́брь
2	Christmas in England	**b**	сентя́брь
3	Dostoevsky born 30 October 1821	**c**	а́вгуст
4	Pushkin born 26 May 1799	**d**	янва́рь
5	Tolstoy born 28 August 1828	**e**	май
6	School year begins 1 September	**f**	дека́брь

The seasons

The Russian words for the seasons bear very little resemblance to their English counterparts (although the first syllable of the English word *autumn* might help you when you're trying to remember the Russian word!).

весна́	spring
ле́то	summer
о́сень	autumn
зима́	winter

Exercise 7.7

Ivan's homework was to name two months for each season, but he has made some mistakes:

1 Which ones has he got right?
2 Sort the others out for him.

1	ВЕСНА	**2**	ЛЕТО
	ию́ль		март
	а́вгуст		апре́ль
3	ОСЕНЬ	**4**	ЗИМА
	сентя́брь		дека́брь
	октя́брь		янва́рь

The illustration is Дед мороз (Grandfather Frost), a close relative of Father Christmas, except that Дед мороз makes his visit on 31 December.

Геогра́фия (Geography)

In a country that spans eleven time zones, the seasons vary considerably, so you need to know whether you'll be in the north, south, east or west. The Russian words for the points of the compass may not sound too familiar at first, but there are ways of helping yourself to remember them:

юг	south	(think of the former Yugoslavia – 'south Slav land')
восто́к	east	(think of Vladivostok in the easternmost part of the Russian Federation)
се́вер	north	(think of the 'severe' weather they have in the north of Russia)
за́пад	west	(this word comes from the idea of the sun setting, or, literally, 'falling' in the west)

In Unit 6 we saw that the endings of Russian words sometimes change, but that this needn't put you off! Look at these next two sentences (and cover up the translation on the right until you've tried to work out the meaning for yourself):

Ло́ндон на ю́ге А́нглии.	*London is in the south of England.*
Арха́нгельск на се́вере Росси́и.	*Arkhangelsk* (Archangel) *is in the north of Russia.*

So, if you want to say *in the north,* etc., you must use the word на in front of the word for *north,* then add the letter 'e' to the end of the word:

на се́вере	*in the north*

Exercise 7.8

Ivan's been struggling with his geography homework on English towns! The sentences on the left are Ivan's. Correct them by completing his teacher's sentences on the right:

ИВАН	УЧИТЕЛЬ (teacher)
1 Лондон на севере.	Нет, Иван, Лондон на ___.
2 Бристоль на востоке.	Нет, Иван, Бристоль на ___.
3 Йорк на юге.	Нет, Иван, Йорк на ___.
4 Ньюкасл на западе.	Нет, Иван, Ньюкасл на ___.
5 Ливерпуль на юге.	Нет, Иван, Ливерпуль на ___.

РУССКИЙ КЛИМАТ (the Russian climate)

Although it does get very cold indeed in many parts of Russia in the winter (−30° and −40° centigrade are not uncommon in some areas), it would be wrong to think that it is always cold everywhere in Russia; temperatures of +40° centigrade can be reached in the summer, even in some parts of Siberia. So here are some key words to describe the weather:

Жарко.	*It is hot.*
Идёт дождь.	*It is raining* (literally, 'walks the rain').
Идёт снег.	*It is snowing* (literally, 'walks the snow').
Холодно.	*It is cold.*

Exercise 7.9

Here are the Russian expressions for *north-east*, etc. Can you work out what they all mean?

1 юго-запад
2 северо-запад
3 юго-восток
4 северо-восток

Insight

Statements about 'how things are' can often be expressed in Russian by one word ending in 'o'. Here are a few examples:

хорошо	*(it's) good*	плохо	*(it's) bad!*
жарко	*it's hot*	холодно	*it's cold*
светло	*it's light*	темно	*it's dark*
интересно	*it's interesting*	скучно	*it's boring*

Exercise 7.10

Look at the map of Russia below.

Now complete the weather forecast below with the appropriate vocabulary or indicate area (e.g. north-west):

На северо-востоке _____. На
_____ идёт дождь. На северо-западе
_____. На юго-западе
_____.

−30°C

Insight

If you want to say *in* a particular season, this is how to do it:

весн**о**й	*in spring*	зим**о**й	*in winter*
л**е**том	*in summer*	**о**сенью	*in autumn*

So, Russian does not use a word for *in* when it is talking about the seasons, but the ending is changed.

Exercise 7.11

Earlier in this unit we met the expression С праздником – best wishes (literally, 'with the celebration'). As well as meaning *celebration*, the word праздник also means *festival* or *holiday*.

In the announcement that follows details are given of a series of festivals, and you will see two words for *festival*: праздник and фестив**а**ль. Once again, don't be put off if the endings of words change!

Праздник русского театра	26 августа
Праздник! Диско-бал (лазерное шоу)	5 сентября
Фестиваль русской музыки	15 сентября
Праздник русского спорта	22 сентября

Which date would you be interested in if you were keen on:

1 sport?
2 music?
3 theatre?
4 disco music?

Insight

To describe bad weather, Russian sometimes uses the word **непог**о**да**. This is made up of the word **не** (*not*) and the word **пог**о**да** (*weather*); in other words, the weather is so bad it's not worth talking about!

End-of-unit review – things to remember, tips and questions

(Answers to the questions are in the Key.)

1 The handwritten я (just like л and м) must start with a little hook.

2 Идёт дождь is the way to say *it's raining*.

3 С днём рождения! means *Happy Birthday!*

4 С Новым годом! means *Happy New Year!*

5 The four points of the compass are: север (*north*), юг (*south*), восток (*east*), запад (*west*).

6 The four seasons are: весна (*spring*), лето (*summer*), осень (*autumn*), зима (*winter*).

7 Work out the meaning of the following three adjectives:

интересный популярный типичный
(Tip! – concentrate on the beginning of each one.)

8 How would you say *pleased to meet you?*

9 What is the Russian word for the season to which these two months belong?

сентябрь, октябрь.

10 If you wanted to say *Hi!* to someone, would you say привет or пока?

Город и транспорт

Town and transport

In this unit you will
- *Consolidate your knowledge of the Cyrillic alphabet*
- *Learn some names of Russian cities*
- *Meet vocabulary on the themes of 'town' and 'transport'*

The word **город** means both *town* and *city*. **Город** appears as part of the name of some Russian towns, e.g. **Новгород** in the north-west of Russia means literally *new town*, even though it is one of Russia's most ancient cities. Founded in the 9th century and known as the 'father' of Russian cities, it is famous for its ancient churches and 14th-century frescoes (**фрески**). An important part of ancient Russian cities was the kremlin (**кремль** – which means *fortress*). The walls of Moscow's **кремль** enclose not just buildings with political and administrative functions, but also some of Russia's most beautiful cathedrals, with their distinctive cupolas (**купола**).

Exercise 8.1

Here is a list of major Russian cities. Put them in alphabetical order:

Омск
Екатеринбу́рг
Тверь
Новосиби́рск
Яку́тск
Москва́
Владивосто́к
Санкт-Петербу́рг
Пермь
Ирку́тск

Russian towns are characterized not only by their kremlins, cupolas and frescoes – the average Russian city is distinguished by its wide streets and high-rise buildings. The majority of Russians live in flats (**кварти́ры** – from the English word *quarters*). The circus (**цирк**) is highly regarded in Russia, and some major cities have their own circus building (a big top would not be appropriate in Russia's climate!); ice-skating and ice-hockey also enjoy great popularity, so an indoor and/or outdoor ice-rink (**като́к**) is standard.

Insight

The Russian unit of currency is the rouble (**рубль**) and this is divided into 100 kopeks (**копейка**). Here are some examples of how you might see prices indicated on items for sale:

700 **рублей**   700 **руб.**   700**р** 50**к**

Exercise 8.2

Look at the list of 'town' vocabulary – buildings you might expect to see in a Russian town. A translation is given only for the words we have not met before. How many of our old friends can you recognize without looking in the Key?

1 банк
2 бассейн   *swimming pool*
3 библиотека
4 больница   *hospital*
5 гостиница
6 департамент
7 каток
8 кинотеатр   *cinema*
9 магазин   *shop*
10 музей   *museum*
11 памятник   *monument*
12 парк   *park*
13 почта
14 ресторан
15 собор   *cathedral*
16 стадион
17 театр
18 улица
19 церковь   *church*
20 цирк

Insight

In Unit 5 we met the word **имени**, which means *of the name* and is often used in the names of a city's important buildings and institutions, e.g.:

Библиот<u>е</u>ка <u>и</u>мени Л<u>е</u>нина	*The Lenin Library*
Институт <u>и</u>мени П<u>у</u>шкина	*The Pushkin Institute*

Exercise 8.3

In the anniversary edition of a theatre programme (below), you will see that the theatre is named after Tchaikovsky:

1 In which two art forms does it specialize?

2 In which city is it situated?

Sight-Seeing

As a tourist visiting a Russian city, you will be interested
to know about the sights that you can visit. Apart from the
very large museums such as the Armoury in Moscow, or the
Hermitage in Saint Petersburg, you will also find smaller
museums which have been created in the buildings formerly
occupied by famous people (e.g. the flats or houses of writers
such as Pushkin, Dostoevsky and Chekhov). Many churches
are now 'working churches', although some, especially the
larger cathedrals, still have museum status. Works of art can
be admired in a gallery or an exhibition hall, and there are
also many palaces to visit, particularly in and around Saint
Petersburg. So, here is a useful vocabulary list for a cultural
visit to a town:

вы́ставочный зал	*exhibition hall*
галере́я	*gallery*
двор<u>е</u>ц	*palace*
дом-муз<u>е</u>й	*house-museum* (i.e. museum housed in building where a famous person lived)
иск<u>у</u>сство	*art*
кварт<u>и</u>ра-муз<u>е</u>й	*flat-museum*
муз<u>е</u>й-соб<u>о</u>р	*museum-cathedral*
Оруж<u>е</u>йная пал<u>а</u>та	*Armoury*
Эрмит<u>а</u>ж	*Hermitage*

Exercise 8.4

Here are the details in English of two tourist groups, followed by
details of two excursions in Moscow:

Group A	Group B
Interested mainly in art and architecture	Interested mainly in literature and music

```
              Экскурсия А2702

                9ч30 отъезд
      10ч30 Большой Кремлёвский дворец
       15ч30 Третьяковская галерея
      18ч30 Лекция «Русское искусство»


              Экскурсия А2902

                14ч30 отъезд
      15ч00 Музей-квартира А.П.Чехова
       17ч00 Лекция «Русская литература»
      19ч30 Опера «Евгений Онегин»
```

1 Which excursion is the appropriate one for group B?
2 Which museum visit is mentioned in Excursion A2902?
3 Where exactly in Moscow is the palace mentioned in Excursion A2702?
4 What activity is on offer at 19.30 in Excursion A2902?

Exercise 8.5

The nine words in the box indicate different buildings in a town:

```
больница          магазин              поликлиника
кинотеатр         медпункт             супермаркет
клуб              парфюмерия           театр
```

1 Which three buildings would you visit if you were making purchases?
2 Which three would you visit if you weren't feeling well?
3 Which three would you visit in your leisure time?

Insight

Город means both *town* and *city*. The five largest cities in the Russian Federation are:

Москва
Санкт-Петербург
Новосибирск
Нижний Новгород
Екатеринбург

At the other end of the scale, the words **село** and **деревня** mean *village*.

Exercise 8.6

Anna has written a postcard below to her friend about her holiday in Moscow. She is keen to recommend the city and mentions four things she has found interesting. What are they? (Don't worry about changes to the endings of words.)

Здесь всё очень интересно—
соборы, музеи, галереи и дворцы.
Одним словом, нам здесь очень
нравится.

Тра́нспорт (Transport)

Of course, you need to be able to get from A to B in a town, so it is important to know what sort of transport is available. Some of the major cities have an underground system, or metro, which is usually the preferred option (and also, in the case of Moscow, worth a visit for the distinctive decorations and sculpture of its stations). If you are travelling by metro, you will need to know where the station is, so you will find a plan of the metro helpful, or just look for a large M as you walk along the street, Every day nearly ten thousand trains run over the system's 12 lines; there are 177 stations, the deepest of which (at 84 metres) is Парк Побе́ды. Russian towns and cities also have buses, trams and trolleybuses. Depending on which city you are visiting, you may need a token (жето́н) or a ticket (биле́т) to travel on public transport. Otherwise, you can always travel by taxi.

Exercise 8.7

Here are the key words discussed in the paragraph you have just read. Can you give the English for each of them?

1 авто́бус
2 биле́т
3 жето́н
4 метро́
5 ста́нция
6 схе́ма метро́
7 такси́
8 трамва́й
9 тра́нспорт
10 тролле́йбус

Travel

If you want to travel by bus, tram or trolleybus, look for a *stop*:
остано́вка

If you want to travel by metro, look for a *station*:
ста́нция

If you want to travel by taxi, look for a *taxi rank*:

стоянка такси

If you're travelling further afield, the train (**поезд**) or plane (**самолёт**) will be needed to cover Russia's vast distances. To catch a train, go to a *station*:

вокзал

The word for *airport* is easiest of all: **аэропорт**.

For most forms of transport the word **поездка** (*journey*) is used. This word is clearly a close relation of **поезд**, but you can use it when you're talking about journeys by metro, bus, tram and trolleybus, too.

Insight

Остановка, станция and стоянка all feature the letters C, T, and H – like the English verb *to stand* (just what you have to do when waiting for a bus, train or taxi!). To remember the word for *railway* station (**вокзал**), think of *Vauxhall* (the source of the Russian word).

Exercise 8.8

Look at the information in the box below, which is taken from a metro ticket:

Билет для проезда в

Московском метрополитена

Не более 60 проездок

Стоимость 150 рублей

---

1 In which city can you use it?
2 How much did it cost?

Exercise 8.9

Here are the names of ten Moscow metro stations:

1 АЭРОПОРТ
2 БИБЛИОТЕКА ИМЕНИ ЛЕНИНА
3 БОТАНИЧЕСКИЙ САД
4 ИЗМАЙЛОВСКИЙ ПАРК
5 КИЕВСКАЯ
6 ПЛОЩАДЬ НОГИНА
7 ПУШКИНСКАЯ
8 ТРЕТЬЯКОВСКАЯ
9 УНИВЕРСИТЕТ
10 ЮГО-ЗАПАДНАЯ

1 Which metro station would you need to go to if you were staying at the Hotel Izmailovskaya?
2 Which station is named after a famous writer?
3 Which station would you go to in order to visit the south-western area of Moscow?
4 Which station would you go to if you were catching a plane?
5 Which station would you go to if you wanted to visit the Tretyakov Art Gallery?

Vocabulary

As we have seen, some words relating to transport have clear western European origins, e.g. some of the public transport just mentioned (*bus, metro, taxi, tram, trolleybus*). We can see this too with some forms of private transport:

автомоби́ль or **маши́на**	*car*
велосипе́д	*bicycle* (the early English form of a bicycle was a 'velocipede' and the French word for 'bicycle' is *vélo*)
мотоци́кл	*motorbike, motorcycle*

Insight

Летать (*to fly*) influences the words for *aeroplane* and *helicopter*, which are good examples of the way Russian builds words from 'roots':

aeroplane = 'a self-flyer': самолёт (сам = self + лёт from *to fly*)

helicopter = 'a turning flyer': вертолёт (верт = turn + лёт from *to fly*).

Exercise 8.10

Which is the only Russian car in the box?

ЛАДА

МЕРСЕДЕС

ПАССАТ

РОУВЕР

ФОРД

Distance

Travelling by train across Russia can be a particularly interesting experience and is a good way to get to meet people, as well as to see the country. A journey to Perm (Пермь) in the Ural mountains, for example, takes approximately 24 hours from Moscow, travelling on the Trans-Siberian Express, which goes on for several days after the Perm passengers have alighted, (or by a 'local' train such as the Кама, which terminates in Perm and is named after the river which flows through that city). Siberia (Сибирь; in Tartar, 'the sleeping land') stretches from the Urals (Урал) to the Pacific (Тихий океан) – a distance of more than 3,000 miles. A ticket or 'travel document' (**проездно̲й докуме̲нт**) for a long-distance journey will probably have the reference:

> РЖД

This is the acronym for Russian Railways (literally, the 'Russian Iron Road' – **росси̲йские желе̲зные доро̲ги**). For a long-distance journey, check the number of your:

ваг**о**н	*carriage*
куп**е**	*compartment*
м**е**сто	*couchette/seat* (literally, *place*)

Exercise 8.11

Look at the travel document, then answer the questions that follow.

ПРОЕЗДНОЙ ДОКУМЕНТ		138465
КАМА	РЖД	ЦЕНА 3500 руб.
Поезд 18 Москва – Пермь 2 Вагон 07 Место 05		Отправление 25.03.10 18.50 Прибытие 26.03.10 15.45

1 How much does the ticket cost?
2 What do you think the word Прибытие might mean?
3 Is 18 the number of the train, the carriage or the compartment?

Exercise 8.12 КРОССВ**О**РД!

ПО ГОРИЗОНТ**А**ЛИ (Across)
1 An airborne vehicle with rotating blades
2 Where you do your shopping
3 The place to keep your money

4 A very large church
5 Sometimes you need one of these instead of a ticket
6 Entertainment involving animals and acrobats
7 An underground railway

ПО ВЕРТИК<u>А</u>ЛИ (Down)
1 Part of a train
2 The place to see plays, opera, ballet
3 A place where you can skate
4 You need to buy one of these in order to travel by bus, plane, train, tram or trolleybus

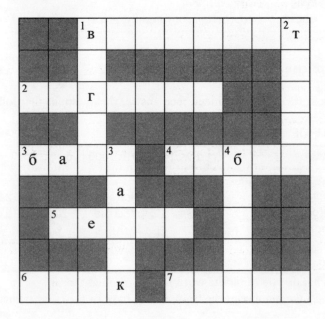

End-of-unit review – questions

(Answers to the questions are in the Key.)

1 If you wanted to swim, which of the following places would you visit?

бассе́йн   библиоте́ка   больни́ца

2 If you wanted to go skating, which of the following places would you visit?

като́к   кинотеа́тр   кремль

3 If you wanted to get a taxi, at which of the following places would you wait?

остано́вка   ста́нция   стоя́нка

4 If you wanted to visit a cathedral, which of the following places would you look for?

собо́р   це́рковь   цирк

5 You have decided to travel by train. Where will you go to catch it?

аэропо́рт   вокза́л   гости́ница

6 Something beginning with З: can you work out what the following three words mean in English?

зе́бра   зо́на   зооло́гия

7 Something beginning with И: can you work out what the following three words mean in English?

инстинкт   интерес   инвестиция

8 Something beginning with Т: can you work out what the following three words mean in English?

телескоп   туннель   тостер

9 Something beginning with Ш: can you work out what the following three words mean in English?

шампунь   шок   шорты

10 Something beginning with Э: can you work out what the following three words mean in English?

энергия   эксплуатация   эмоция

9

Гости́ница и рестора́н
Hotel and restaurant

In this unit you will
- *Have more practice in reading the Cyrillic alphabet*
- *Learn how to count in Russian*
- *Meet some useful vocabulary about hotels and restaurants*

Russia's larger cities have a large selection of hotels, with comprehensive websites. Here are some typical hotel names from Russia's three largest cities (Moscow, St Petersburg and Novosibirsk); as you will see, names of places, regions and rivers are prominent:

Балти́йская	*Baltic*
Бородино́	*Borodino* (site of the famous battle in 1812 between Napoleon's troops and the Imperial Russian army)
Во́лга	*Volga* (river)
Восто́к	*East*
Комфо́рт	*Comfort*
Ко́смос	*Cosmos*
Нева́	*Neva* (river in St Petersburg)
Пётр Пе́рвый	*Peter I* (Peter the Great)
Сиби́рь	*Siberia*
Тури́ст	*Tourist*

On arrival at your hotel, you will register with the администратор (*administrator*) and get your ключ (*key*) or your карта-ключ (*key card*); it is usual for the guests on each floor of a hotel to be looked after by the дежурная (*lady on duty*).

Exercise 9.1

Here is a list of 'hotel' vocabulary. A translation is given only for the words we have not met before. How many of our old friends can you recognize without looking in the Key (or Unit 6, where we first met them)?

1	администратор	
2	бланк	
3	виза	
4	горничная	*maid*
5	гостиница	
6	дежурная	*lady on duty, responsible for floor of hotel*
7	ключ	*key*
8	номер	
9	паспорт	
10	этаж	

Hotels in Russia's major cities tend to be very large and they specialize in both tourism and business. Here are some words describing hotel facilities to add to those you met in Unit 6:

бассейн	*swimming pool*
боулинг	*bowling*
бутики	*boutiques*
казино	*casino*
лифт	*lift*
парикмахерская	*hairdresser's*
ремонт	*repairs*
салон красоты	*beauty salon*
фитнес-центр	*fitness centre*
химчистка	*dry cleaning*

Рем<u>о</u>нт is a repair service (e.g. for shoes), but it also means *repair*. You may see this sign in your hotel:

If you do, you will know that the facility in question is *closed for repair*.

Exercise 9.2

Look at the the information given below.

> САНКТ-ПЕТЕРБУРГ
>
> ПЛОЩАДЬ АЛЕКСАНДРА НЕВСКОГО, 2
>
> # ГОСТИНИЦА МОСКВА
>
> В центре города – Метро «Площадь Александра Невского» тел (812) 333-2-444

1 Why is this a very convenient hotel for the tourist?
2 What useful information does it give about how to get to the hotel?

Vocabulary

We have met the word **пл<u>о</u>щадь** (*square*) twice:

Кр<u>а</u>сная пл<u>о</u>щадь	*Red Square*
Пл<u>о</u>щадь Алекс<u>а</u>ндра Н<u>е</u>вского	*Aleksandr Nevsky Square*

The original meaning of **Кр<u>а</u>сная пл<u>о</u>щадь** was *beautiful square* (so it has nothing to do with the red banners of Communism).

Площадь Александра Невского is named after Aleksandr Nevsky, who is renowned for his victory over the Swedes in the 13th century. The main street in Saint Petersburg is also named after him (**Невский проспект**).

You can practise recognition of Cyrillic by visiting hotel websites; some sites offer a **виртуальный тур** (*virtual tour*) of rooms and facilities. Room types include the following (in ascending price order!):

стандарт	*standard*
комфорт	*comfort*
люкс	*luxury*
люкс плюс	*luxury plus*

One of the services usually available in large hotels is foreign currency exchange. The key words in this context are:

обмен	*exchange*
валюта	*foreign currency* (Remember? It sounds like 'value'.)

If you are changing money in a hotel, you will receive a record of your transaction, on which the cashier will indicate the sum exchanged and the amount of roubles received in words (not necessarily in figures). Here are some Russian numerals:

1 один	11 одиннадцать	30 тридцать	400 четыреста
2 два	12 двенадцать	40 сорок	500 пятьсот
3 три	13 тринадцать	50 пятьдесят	600 шестьсот
4 четыре	14 четырнадцать	60 шестьдесят	700 семьсот
5 пять	15 пятнадцать	70 семьдесят	800 восемьсот
6 шесть	16 шестнадцать	80 восемьдесят	900 девятьсот
7 семь	17 семнадцать	90 девяносто	1,000 тысяча
8 восемь	18 восемнадцать	100 сто	
9 девять	19 девятнадцать	200 двести	
10 десять	20 двадцать	300 триста	

'Compound' numbers (e.g. 24, 55, 103) are easy in
Russian – just place one number after the other:

24	двадцать четыре
55	пятьдесят пять
103	сто три

Insight

Ten is **десять**, and you can help yourself to remember this
by thinking of *decimal*. You might find it helpful to think
of **двенадцать** (*12*) as '2 on 10' (**на** = *on*, and – **дцать** is
from **десять**) and **двадцать** (*20*) as 'two tens' (**два** and –
дцать).

Exercise 9.3

Here are some details from a currency exchange form at a bank in
a Russian hotel. Look at it, then answer (in English) the questions
below:

СПРАВКА БУ	ПУНКТ ОБМЕНА ВАЛЮТ 08908809
	гостиница «Достоевский»
	Москва
	ул Владимирский, д. 19
Клиент (фамилия)	Грант, М.
Резидент_____	Нерезидент_____✓_____
Сумма тридцать долларов США	
Получено клиентом	тысяча пятьсот рублей
23 марта 2010г	

1 In which hotel is the exchange bank situated?
2 What is the client's surname?
3 Is the client resident in the hotel?

4 What sum of money is being exchanged?
5 How many roubles does the client receive?
6 What is the date of the transaction?

Insight

Hotels usually give useful information about the nearest metro stations, or the distance from the airport/city centre. Look out for expressions such as:

5	**мин. пешком** (*five minutes on foot*)
20	**мин. езды от аэропорта** (*a twenty-minute journey from the airport*)

Exercise 9.4

Look at the hotel card below:

> ГОСТИНИЦА «ДОСТОЕВСКИЙ»
>
> в историческом центре города
>
> Владимирский, д. 19
>
> метро «Достоевский» (2 мин. пешком)
>
> Во всех номерах гостиницы «Достоевский» мини-бар, спутниковое ТВ, телефон, кондиционер, санузел (ванна/душ).

1 In which particular part of St Petersburg is the hotel situated?
2 How far is it from the nearest metro station?
3 Can you identify some of the items offered in each room? (Во всех номер**а**х – *in all rooms*)

Food

If you visit the hotel's **буфет**, you are likely to have the choice of a selection of sandwiches and drinks:

бутерброд	*sandwich*
водка	*vodka*
коньяк	*cognac*
кофе	*coffee*
минеральная вода	*mineral water*
чай	*tea*

A main meal in a restaurant, on the other hand, would be composed of a series of courses. First you'll want to consult the menu (**меню**) and then place your order with the waiter (**официант**) or the waitress (**официантка**) – unless your set meals are part of a package. Starters (**закуски**) are a much more substantial course than in western Europe and might include salads, cold meats, smoked fish, small pasties and open sandwiches; this is followed by soup (**суп**), then a hot meat or fish course. The most usual desserts are fruit compote or ice cream. Bread (**хлеб**) is a very important component of any Russian meal, and black (rye) bread is the most traditional: **чёрный хлеб**.

Exercise 9.5

The waiter in your restaurant is having trouble sorting out who has ordered what. You are with two friends who have ordered a light lunch and fortunately you jotted down what each of you chose. Here is your list:

Viktor:	soup, omelette, mineral water
Tanya:	salad, bread and wine
You:	soup, salad, bread, wine

Now here's what the waiter actually brings for you:

Ви́ктор:	суп, сала́т, вино́
Та́ня:	минера́льная вода́, омле́т, хлеб
Ты:	суп, омле́т, вино́, хлеб

What mistakes has the waiter made?

Mealtime! The three meals of the day are:

за́втрак	*breakfast* (in large hotels now often served on a self-service basis from a Swedish table – шве́дский стол)
обе́д	*lunch* (often the most substantial meal of the day)
у́жин	*supper*

Insight

За́втрак (*breakfast*) is related to the word за́втра, which means *tomorrow*. Второ́й за́втрак literally means *second breakfast* – i.e. *mid-morning snack*, *"elevenses"*. You can make a verb from all of the words indicating a meal:

за́втракать – *to (have) breakfast*
обе́дать – *to (have) lunch*
у́жинать – *to have supper*

Exercise 9.6

The excursion programme for the day is rather complicated:

08ч00	за́втрак (гости́ница «Бороди́но», рестора́н А)
09ч00	отъе́зд
10ч30	Кремль и Кра́сная пло́щадь

12ч00	обед (гостиница «Космос», шведский стол)
14ч00	Исторический музей
18ч00	ужин (гостиница «Мелодия», буфет этаж 5)
19ч30	Большой театр

1 Which meal will you be eating in the Hotel Borodino?
2 What sort of lunch will the Hotel Cosmos be providing?
3 What will you be visiting before lunch?
4 Where are you going after supper?

Typical Russian food

блин	*pancake*
икра	*caviar*
квас	*kvass* (a drink made from fermented rye bread)
сметана	*sour cream*

Soup is considered to be a hugely important part of the Russian diet; hot soups to give warmth in the cold of winter, but also cold, spicy soups in the intense heat of a southern Russian summer. The most well known of the hot soups are: борщ (*beetroot soup*) – although mushroom борщ with prunes can also be served cold – and щи (*cabbage soup*). Other Russian soups include солянка (a spicy meat and vegetable soup with dill-pickled cucumbers) and окрошка (a cold soup made with kvass or cider).

Insight

An example of щи (*cabbage soup*) in a Russian proverb:

The Russian equivalent of 'to get into hot water' literally means to end up like a cock in the cabbage soup: попасть (*to get into/end up*) как (*like*) кур (*a cock*) во (*into/in*) щи (*cabbage soup*).

Exercise 9.7

Guests at a Saint Petersburg hotel have been asked to fill in a questionnaire about the hotel's services. They have been asked to give their assessment under three categories:

отлично   *excellent*
хорошо   *OK*
плохо   *bad*

Служьа means *service*, and приём (*reception*) can make an important first impression on new guests! Look at the form of one guest, then answer the questions which follow:

	ОТЛИЧНО	ХОРОШО	ПЛОХО
служба приёма (администратор)			✓
служба этажа (дежурная)		✓	
рестораны	✓		
буфеты и кафетерии	✓		
бары	✓		
ремонт, стирка, химчистка		✓	
Дата заполнения: 19 ноября 2010			

1 Which is the only form of service the guest found to be poor?
2 Which things were found to be excellent?
3 When did the guest complete this form?

Exercise 9.8

You have just received a postcard from your Russian friend, who is on holiday in Saint Petersburg. Look for the key words to answer the following questions. (You might need to revise some of the weather vocabulary in Unit 7.)

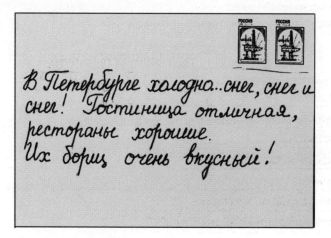

В Петербурге холодно…снег, снег и снег! Гостиница отличная, рестораны хорошие. Их борщ очень вкусный!

1 What is the weather like?
2 What is the hotel like?
3 What food does she mention?

End-of-unit review – questions

(Answers to the questions are in the Key.)

1 The word услуги means *services*. What kind of services are on offer in a hotel if you see this sign?

секрет<u>а</u>рские усл<u>у</u>ги

2 If you wanted a haircut, which sign would you follow – парикм<u>а</u>херская or рем<u>о</u>нт?

3 If you wanted to buy some souvenirs, which hotel kiosk would you visit – сувен<u>и</u>рный ки<u>о</u>ск or апт<u>е</u>чный ки<u>о</u>ск?

4 You see the following sign in your hotel – театр<u>а</u>льные бил<u>е</u>ты. What is on offer?

5 What is on offer in the sports complex?

аэр<u>о</u>бика   <u>а</u>ква-аэр<u>о</u>бика   джак<u>у</u>зи

6 What leisure activities are available here?

билья<u>я</u>рд   дартс   кара<u>о</u>ке

7 What goods are on sale at the boutique in the beauty salon?

бут<u>и</u>к с косм<u>е</u>тикой и аксессу<u>а</u>рами

8 The beauty salon offers these three services; what are they?

масс<u>а</u>ж   маник<u>ю</u>р   педик<u>ю</u>р

9 How many floors are there in this hotel?

пятн<u>а</u>дцать

10 How many rooms are there in the hotel?

тр<u>и</u>ста дв<u>а</u>дцать

Хо̲бби
Hobbies

In this unit you will
- *Revise all the letters of the Cyrillic alphabet*
- *Meet some useful vocabulary about sport and other hobbies*

Part 1 (Ча̲сть пе̲рвая)

Sport (Спорт) enjoys great popularity in Russia. Some of the more popular forms of sport are related to the country's climate, for example:

КАТА̲НИЕ НА ЛЫ̲ЖАХ	*skiing*
ФИГУ̲РНОЕ КАТА̲НИЕ	*figure skating*
ХОККЕ̲Й (НА ЛЬДУ)	*ice hockey*

In fact, when you're talking about hockey in Russia, ice hockey will be assumed. Another favourite in Russia is fishing (ры̲бная ло̲вля), and in the depths of winter you will see fishermen sitting by holes they have drilled in the thick ice of frozen rivers. Swimmers, too, are undaunted by the rigours of winter – in Moscow there are about 3,500 *walruses* (моржи̲), intrepid swimmers who dig out areas in the ice so that they can swim outdoors all year round. There are 'walrus clubs' all over Russia, and members are of all ages (with some in their eighties); their favourite air temperature for swimming (плавание) is −20° centigrade. The water temperature is apparently significantly warmer (especially near the river bed), but the walruses still emerge with icicles in their hair.

Exercise 10.1

Only one of the sports listed does not involve water. Which is it?

1 се́рфинг
2 пла́вание
3 виндсе́рфинг
4 баскетбо́л
5 ры́бная ло́вля

Vocabulary

A key verb involved with sport is 'to play': игра́ть. The words linked to this (*game*, *play*, *player*) are easy to recognize because they all clearly have the same 'root' (i.e. they all start with игр):

игра́	*game, play (in the sense of playing, performing)*
игра́ть	*to play*
игро́к	*player*

Sometimes you can learn two words 'for the price of one'; so, in the case of *to play*, there are second meanings:

игра́ть	*to gamble*
игро́к	*gambler*

This kind of 'family grouping' of vocabulary is very common in Russian, so if you don't recognize a new word, it's always worth trying to work out what it means by looking for a root. In sporting vocabulary the groups work in very much the same way:

футбо́л	*football*
футболи́ст	*footballer*

футбо́льный матч	football match
хокке́й	hockey
хокке́ист	hockey player
хокке́йный матч	hockey match

The *football* root also provides us with the Russian word for a T-shirt: футбо́лка.

Not all words associated with sport are so easily recognizable; although some you might be able to recognize by association, e.g. альпини́зм (*mountaineering* – think of the Alps), but others are really not very obvious:

борьба́	wrestling
го́нки	motor racing
пла́вание	swimming
прыжо́к в длину́	long jump
фехтова́ние	fencing

The word for a *fan* in Russian is боле́льщик, which comes from the Russian word for *to be ill*: боле́ть – in other words being a fan indicates a degree of obsession with your team. You might want to watch your team (кома́нда) live at the stadium (стадио́н) or in the comfort of your own home, on the television (по телеви́зору).

Ката́ние literally means *rolling* and it is used to describe a range of sporting activities, e.g.:

ката́ние верхо́м	(horse) riding
ката́ние на конька́х	skating
ката́ние на ло́дке	boating
ката́ние на лы́жах	skiing
ката́ние на ро́ликах	roller-skating
ката́ние на саня́х	sledging, tobogganing
фигу́рное ката́ние	figure skating

Exercise 10.2

Read this little paragraph about Sergei and answer the English questions which follow (don't worry if you don't understand all the words – you'll still be able to answer the questions):

Сергей – хоккеист. Он играет в хоккей на стадионе. Сергей играет в хоккей по средам и по субботам. Сергей не играет в футбол, но он любит смотреть футбол по телевизору.

1 Which sport does Sergei play at the stadium?
2 On which days of the week does he play?
3 Which sport does he watch on television?

Exercise 10.3

Match the sports in the left-hand list with the people who play them in the right-hand list. Hunt for 'roots' to help you.

1	волейбол	**А**	гимнаст
2	гольф	**Б**	пловец
3	плавание	**В**	фехтовальщик
4	борьба	**Г**	игрок в гольф
5	гимнастика	**Д**	гонщик
6	прыжок в длину	**Е**	борец
7	альпинизм	**Ж**	прыгун
8	фехтование	**З**	волейболист
9	крикет	**И**	альпинист
10	гонки	**К**	игрок в крикет

Insight

Here are some sayings based on **играть** (*to play*):

играть в ко́шки-мы́шки (ко́шки = *cats*; мы́шки = *small mice*) – 'to exploit an advantageous position over someone else', *to play a cat-and-mouse game*

играть втору́ю скри́пку (втору́ю = *second*; скри́пку = *violin*) – 'to have a less important position', *to play second fiddle*

Exercise 10.4

Where would you be able to participate in all these various sports? Choose the appropriate word for each sport from the box.

1 Tennis
2 Figure skating
3 Football
4 Swimming
5 Volleyball

Notice the word площадка (pitch, ground; literally, little square), a close relation of the word for *square* (площадь) which we met in Unit 9 (e.g. *Red Square* – Красная площадь).

Hobbies (Хобби)

Sports programmes on television are also extremely popular, especially if it is a **футбольный матч** or a **хоккейный матч**.

Popular names for teams (not just in Moscow) are Dynamo (**Динамо**), Torpedo (**Торпедо**) and Spartak (**Спартак**).

Not all leisure activities are connected with sport. Look at this list of other leisure activities. How many can you recognize without looking at the list on the right?

кино	*cinema*
компьютерные игры	*computer games*
музыка	*music*

театр	*theatre*
телевизионные программы	*television programmes*
шахматы	*chess*

Not all leisure vocabulary is so user-friendly. The following are not at all like their English counterparts:

| рисование | *drawing, painting* |
| чтение | *reading* |

The word for *chess* (шахматы) is initially not very recognizable, but once you realize it comes from *checkmate* you'll find it easy to remember.

The Russian words for some more recent pursuits are clearly based on their English counterparts (e.g. картинг – *go-karting*), while others have adopted new English forms (for example, a motorbike enthusiast could now be called байкер instead of мотоциклист).

Exercise 10.5

The following list of words needs to be sorted out under three headings: 1 Musical/Dramatic; 2 Sport; 3 Other. Which words will go under which heading?

А Балет		**Е** Шекспир «Ромео и Джульетта»
Б Шахматы		**Ж** Атлетика
В Телесериал		**З** Чтение
Г Хоккейный матч		**И** Оркестр
Д Опера		**К** Гол

Insight

The names of most musical instruments resemble their English counterparts; e.g.:

| виолончель | *cello* |
| кларнет | *clarinet* |

саксоф<u>о</u>н	*saxophone*
тромб<u>о</u>н	*trombone*
фл<u>е</u>йта	*flute*

Some have a more onomatopaeic derivation! The word
скр<u>и</u>пка (*violin*) comes from the verb **скрип<u>е</u>ть** (*to squeak, creak*), whilst **бараб<u>а</u>н** (*drum*) has a pleasingly percussive sound!

....

Exercise 10.6

The two advertisements (А and Б) are incomplete. The graphics still have to be added.

1 Which box will the artist put drawing 1 into?
2 And drawing 2?
3 Where is the activity in Box A to take place?
4 For which day of the week is the activity in Box Б scheduled?

1   **2**

А

ЧЕТВЕРГ 10 ДЕКАБРЯ

ЛЕКЦИЯ «Компьютер – друг или враг?»

(Университет, 17ч30)

Б

СУББОТА 19 ДЕКАБРЯ

ВЫСТАВКА «Лучшие телесериалы нашего века»

(Библиотека, 09ч00–18ч00)

Exercise 10.7

You have just received a postcard from your Russian friend
Igor listing the activities on offer on his holiday. Look for the
key words in it which will help you to answer the following
questions:

1 Which two sporting activities are on offer?
2 What can the 'non-sporty' do?
3 Which resort is Igor staying in?

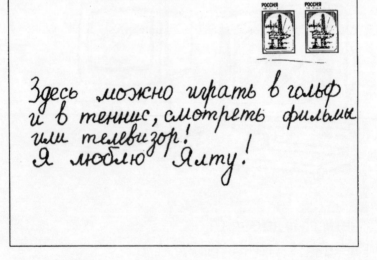

Здесь можно играть в гольф
и в теннис, смотреть фильмы
или телевизор!
Я люблю Ялту!

Insight

The contemporary music scene features many words derived from English:

поп	*pop*
рок	*rock*
рэп	*rap*
р<u>е</u>тро	*retro*

Names of groups and bands also reflect Western European influences (**Динам<u>и</u>т, Мир<u>а</u>ж, Смэш!**), though some opt for Russian names: **Р<u>у</u>ки вверх!** (*Hands up!*), **Серебр<u>о</u>** (*Silver*), **Ф<u>а</u>брика** (*Factory*).

Exercise 10.8

You have just received a card (overleaf) inviting you to a 70th anniversary concert at a music school.

1 In which city is the concert to take place?
2 After which composer is the school named?

Exercise 10.9

Rimsky-Korsakov, one of Russia's most famous composers, was also a leading teacher and conductor. Look at the information about him in Russian. Can you identify the words for: composer, conductor, symphonies and suites?

Никола́й Андре́евич Ри́мский-Ко́рсаков (1844–1908) – компози́тор (о́перы, симфо́нии, сю́иты) педаго́г, дирижёр.

Insight

Some Russian time words – try pronouncing them: **утро** (*morning*), **в<u>е</u>чер** (*evening*), **ночь** (*night*). There is no specific word for *afternoon*; one of the ways of expressing this is to say **после об<u>е</u>да** (*after lunch*). Take care with the word for *today* – **сег<u>о</u>дня**: the Г is pronounced as a 'v' (syev<u>o</u>dnya).

Part 2 (Ч<u>а</u>сть втор<u>а</u>я)

And now for some general practice!

Exercise 10.10

You are trying to decide which restaurant to eat at. Don't be put off that you don't know all the words in the three adverts – you can still find the information you need.

Ресторан А

> **ПАТИО ПАСТА**
>
> Итальянская еда в центре Москвы. Открыт с 12 дня до 12 ночи.

Ресторан Б

> **ДАНИЛОВСКИЙ**
>
> Традиционная русская кухня. Элегантная обстановка. Открыт до 11 вечера.

Ресторан B

СЕВИЛЛИЯ

Испанский ресторан. Широкий выбор вин. Открыт до
5 утра.

1 Which restaurant specializes in traditional Russian dishes?
2 Which is offering Italian food?
3 Which one would you choose if you wanted Spanish food?
4 Which one recommends its fine wines?
5 Which one claims to have an elegant setting?
6 Which one has a central location?

Exercise 10.11

The following announcement explains the procedure for using
credit cards. Here's some vocabulary to help you answer the
questions:

и́ли	*or*
име́ть	*to have, possess*
на́до	*it is necessary*
принима́ются	*are accepted*

1 In which three places can a credit card be used?
2 What else must you present with your credit card in order to
use it?

КРЕДИТНЫЕ КАРТОЧКИ

Кредитные карточки
принимаются в гостиницах,
ресторанах и казино. Надо
иметь паспорт или
идентификацию.

Exercise 10.12

Which of the following is not a form of transport? What is it?

1	самолёт	**6**	трамва́й
2	авто́бус	**7**	бо́дибилдинг
3	байк	**8**	метро́
4	велосипе́д	**9**	по́езд
5	вертолёт	**10**	тролле́йбус

Exercise 10.13

Look at the floor guide of a large department store, then answer the questions:

ЭТАЖ	ОТДЕЛ
1	Книги, журналы, газеты
2	Багаж – рюкзаки, сумки, чемоданы
3	Телевизоры, компьютерная техника, плееры и рекордеры
4	Кафе-ресторан, туалеты
5	Музыка – ноты, компактные диски
6	Мода, парфюмерия, Салон Красоты

1 On which floor could you get something to eat?
2 Which floor specializes in computer goods?
3 Which floor would you go to if you wanted something to read?
4 Where could you buy some perfume?
5 Where would you go to buy luggage?

Exercise 10.14

You're checking through receipts from the exchange bank. Try to make out the amount of money changed by each client. The amounts are written in words, so you might find it helpful to look back to Unit 9.

Клиент А

Сумма	<u>двадцать долларов США</u>
Получено клиентом	<u>шестьсот рублей</u>
27 февраля 2010г	

Клиент Б

Сумма	<u>двадцать английских фунтов</u> <u>стерлингов</u>
Получено клиентом	<u>восемьсот рублей</u>
12 апреля 2010г	

Клиент В

Сумма	<u>двадцать канадских долларов</u>
Получено клиентом	<u>пятьсот семьдесят пять рублей</u>
22 июня 2010г	

Клиент Г

Сумма	<u>двадцать евро</u>
Получено клиентом	<u>восемьсот двадцать пять рублей</u>
7 июля 2010г	

1 Which client changed money in June?
2 What sort of currency did this client change?
3 How many roubles did Клиент Б receive?
4 What sort of currency did Клиент Г change?

Exercise 10.15 КРОССВ<u>О</u>РД!

This final crossword draws on your knowledge of the vocabulary and on some of the 'cultural background' you have learnt during the units.

ПО ГОРИЗОНТ<u>А</u>ЛИ (Across)

1 The most famous one is in Moscow, but many cities have one. (It means 'fortress'.)
2 Important to know which one your hotel room is on
3 A secretary works in one.
4 The place to visit if you're interested in history
5 If you like go-karting, you'll want one of these.
6 The male version of sister
7 A musician plays in one.
8 The country where people speak Russian

ПО ВЕРТИК<u>А</u>ЛИ (Down)

1 This festival takes place in January in Russia.
2 Third month of the year
3 This person works in a restaurant.
4 An essential part of the Russian diet
5 A person who writes books
6 A very popular food in China

End-of-unit review – questions

(Answers to the questions are in the Key.)

Use the vocabulary list which follows this unit to help you (all good reading practice!).

1 Find the odd one out:

омл<u>е</u>т те<u>а</u>тр м<u>у</u>зыка <u>о</u>пера

2 Find the odd one out:

виндс<u>е</u>рфинг парк т<u>е</u>ннис футб<u>о</u>л

3 Find the odd one out:

университ<u>е</u>т   снег   студ<u>е</u>нт   проф<u>е</u>ссор

4 Find the odd one out:

рот   нос   <u>а</u>вгуст   голов<u>а</u>

5 Find the odd one out:

<u>о</u>фис   мать   сын   дочь

6 If you were a tourist interested in history, which of these places would you want to visit?

a сто<u>я</u>нка такс<u>и</u>   **b** муз<u>е</u>й   **c** басс<u>е</u>йн

7 Where would a waiter be most likely to work?

a больн<u>и</u>ца   **b** банк   **c** ресто<u>а</u>н

8 What would you have to buy if you wanted to go to the theatre?

a бил<u>е</u>т   **b** баг<u>а</u>ж   **c** чемод<u>а</u>н

9 If you were a tourist, where would you want to stay?

a цирк   **b** <u>це</u>рковь   **c** гост<u>и</u>ница

10 If you were hungry, which of the following would be appropriate?

a хлеб   **b** шарф   **c** н<u>о</u>мер

Key to the exercises

Unit 1

1.1
1 b atom, **2 e** cat, **3 a** tact, **4 d** coma, **5 c** cocoa
1.2
5 КАМА
1.4
1 Who is there? **2** Yes
Мак – the name of the Scotsman that means *poppy* in Russian
1.5
1 как, **2** там, **3** кто, **4** так
End-of-unit review questions: 6 а, **7** о, **8** кто, **9** там, **10** как

Unit 2

2.1
Нева
2.3
1 р, **2** е, **3** к, **4** а, **5** река
2.4
1 е, **2** h, **3** g, **4** i, **5** b, **6** d, **7** j, **8** а, **9** f, **10** с
2.5
1 к, **2** р, **3** е, **4** с, **5** т, **6** крест
2.6
нота, оркестр, рок, тенор, тон
End-of-unit review questions: 7 here/there is/are, **8** нет,
9 касса, **10** Москва

Unit 3

3.1
1 c, **2** d, **3** a, **4** b
3.2
1 а в_о_дка (vodka), **2** в банк (bank), **3** б Гонк_о_нг (Hong Kong), **4** в трамв_а_й (tram)
3.3
1 с, **2** и, **3** в, **4** д, **5** а, **6** г, **7** л, **8** р, **9** з, **10** в
3.4
баскетб_о_л, волейб_о_л, футб_о_л
3.5
1 Ouch! My ear aches! **2** Ouch! My tooth aches!
3.6
1 c, **2** f, **3** e, **4** b, **5** d, **6** a
3.7
1 America, **2** Argentina, **3** Africa, **4** Mexico, **5** Canada, **6** Cyprus, **7** Cuba, **8** Pakistan, **9** Uganda, **10** Ukraine
End-of-unit review questions: 7 committee, complex, contact; **8** lavender, lift, literature; **9** megabite, microbe, million; **10** parasite, port, portrait

Unit 4

4.3
Яп_о_ния (Japan)
4.4
К_а_тя
4.7
джаз (jazz; the other activities are windsurfing, ping-pong, cards and Scrabble)
4.9
лимон_а_д
4.10
1 Валент_и_н, **2** В_и_ктор

4.11

1 grandson,　**2** Ольга and Зоя,　**3** Константи́новна

4.12

1 October,　**2** Paganini and Rachmaninov,　**3** Nikolai Baikov

And for a translation of the programme:

> **Theatre of opera and ballet**
>
> **CONCERT**
>
> **30 October (at 12 o'clock)**
>
> Paganini
> Concerto No. 1 for Violin and Orchestra
> Soloist Aleksander Chirkov
> Rachmaninov
> Concerto No. 2 for Piano and Orchestra
> Soloist Nikolai Baikov

4.13

Космона́вт (astronaut, cosmonaut) is the odd one out.

Russian	Meaning
банк	*bank*
креди́т	*credit*
креди́тная ка́рточка	*credit card*
инвести́ция	*investment*
фина́нсовый кри́зис	*financial crisis*
космона́вт	*astronaut*
до́ллары	*dollars*
эконо́мика	*economics*
капита́л	*capital*
банки́р	*banker*

End-of-unit review questions:　**7** risk, ritual, routine;　**8** server (*computer*), scandal, snob;　**9** television channel, test, trophy; **10** final (*sport*), finale (*show*), focus-group, formula

Unit 5

5.1
1 b, **2** g, **3** e, **4** a
5.2
a footballer, **b** nurse, **c** hockey player, **d** engineer, **e** ballerina,
f journalist, **g** jockey, **h** pianist
5.3
1 supermarket, **2** actress, **3** 9 p.m. (21.00)
5.4
1 он, **2** он<u>а</u>
5.5
1 космон<u>а</u>вт, **2** хокке<u>и</u>ст, **3** пиан<u>и</u>ст
5.6
1 f, **2** c, **3** h, **4** l, **5** a, **6** d, **7** g, **8** k, **9** j, **10** b,
11 i, **12** e
5.7
1 Thursday, **2** Friday, **3** Tuesday, **4** Sunday, **5** Monday,
6 Wednesday, **7** Saturday
5.8
Correct alphabetical order is:
Бармина
Вереев
Грязнова
Давыдов
Кондратов
Лев
Носиков
Селезнев
Туманова
Хоботова
There are four women in the group – **Бармина, Грязнова, Туманова,
Хоботова**.

5.9

Correct alphabetical order is: АВТОЦЕНТР, АНТИКВАРИАТ, БИЗНЕС, КОМПЬЮТЕРЫ, ТАЙМШЕР, ТЕЛЕВИЗОРЫ.

1 АВТОЦЕНТР, **2** АНТИКВАРИАТ, **3** ТАЙМШЕР, **4** КОМПЬЮТЕРЫ, **5** БИЗНЕС

5.10

1 Соня, **2** Анна, **3** Максим, **4** дедушка, **5** бабушка

5.11

1 Tchaikovsky, **2** Row 5, **3** 19.30

5.12

Формула-1 is not a school subject. If this list were in alphabetical order, the first word would be **география**, and the last would be **химия**.

End-of-unit review questions: 7 demonstration, diet, designer; **8** idea, isolation/insulation, inspector; **9** cement, centre, cycle/series; **10** нерв (*nerve*), ноутбук (*computer: laptop, notebook*), организм (*organism*), стресс (*stress*), субъект (*subject*), юмор (*humour*)

Unit 6

6.2

4 май (May)

6.3

1 c, **2** e, **3** a, **4** b, **5** d

6.4

4 Рахманинов (Rachmaninov) is a composer; all the others are writers.

6.5

1 A=travel agent; B=estate agent, **2** office, fitness centre, car park (for 50 cars); class A (1st class), **3** Australia (windsurfing and surfing), Austria (coach/bus tours), Africa (national park safaris)

		¹г	и	д		
		о				
²п	а	с	п	о	р	т
		т				
	³в	и	з	а		
		н				
	⁴б	и	л	е	²т	
		ц			е	
		а			а	
					т	
	⁵н	о	м	е	р	

6.7
1 b, **2** d, **3** h (literally, 'medical point'), **4** g (literally, 'militia'), **5** f, **6** a, **7** e, **8** c

6.8
1 Norway, **2** Italy, **3** Canada, **4** England, **5** Finland,
6 Holland, **7** Ukraine, **8** Austria, **9** France, **10** Australia

6.9
1 2488, **2** 2549, **3** 2027, **4** 2nd, **5** 2nd, **6** 1st

6.10
1 Crime, Autobiography, Humour, Biography, Historical romance,
2 Автобиогра́фия, Биогра́фия, Детекти́в, Истори́ческий
рома́нтизм, Ю́мор

End-of-unit review questions: 7 врач, **8** по́чта, **9** вы́ход,
10 экза́мен, экску́рсия, экспе́рт, элега́нтный, э́то

Unit 7

7.2
5 ш<u>а</u>хматы (chess)
7.3
1 о   **2** р   **3** з   **4** н   **5** и
7.4
1 р,   **2** о,   **3** з,   **4** а The missing letters give the word р<u>о</u>за (*rose*).
7.5
Popular medicine, Russian history, Russian literature, Russian music,
scandals
7.6
1 d,   **2** f,   **3** a,   **4** e,   **5** c,   **6** b
7.7
1 Autumn and winter are correct.   **2** He has got the months under
spring and summer the wrong way round. They should be:

1   ВЕСНА   **2**   ЛЕТО
    март   и<u>ю</u>ль
    апр<u>е</u>ль   <u>а</u>вгуст

7.8
1 <u>ю</u>ге,   **2** з<u>а</u>паде,   **3** с<u>е</u>вере,   **4** вост<u>о</u>ке,   **5** с<u>е</u>вере
7.9
1 south-west,   **2** north-west,   **3** south-east,   **4** north-east
7.10
1 идёт снег,   **2** <u>ю</u>го-вост<u>о</u>ке,   **3** х<u>о</u>лодно,   **4** ж<u>а</u>рко
7.11
1 22 September,   **2** 15 September,   **3** 26 August,   **4** 5 September
End-of-unit review questions: **7** interesting, popular, typical;
8 <u>О</u>чень при<u>я</u>тно!   **9** <u>о</u>сень,   **10** прив<u>е</u>т

Unit 8

8.1
Владивост<u>о</u>к
Екатеринб<u>у</u>рг
Ирк<u>у</u>тск
Москв<u>а</u>

Новосибирск
Омск
Пермь
Санкт-Петербург
Тверь
Якутск

8.2

1 bank, **3** library, **5** hotel, **6** department, **7** ice-rink,
8 Кинотеатр is the building; кино is either the building or the film medium, **13** post office, **14** restaurant, **16** stadium,
17 theatre, **18** street, **20** circus

8.3

1 opera and ballet, **2** Perm (Пермь)

8.4

1 A2902, **2** Chekhov's flat, **3** Kremlin, **4** the opera *Evgeny Onegin*

8.5

(Translations only given for words we have not met before.)
1 магазин деликатесов delicatessen; парфюмерия perfumery; супермаркет supermarket, **2** больница; медпункт first-aid post; literally, medical point; поликлиника clinic, **3** кинотеатр; клуб; театр

8.6

соборы, музеи, галереи и дворцы (cathedrals, museums, galleries and palaces)

8.7

1 bus, **2** ticket, **3** token, **4** metro, **5** station, **6** metro plan, **7** taxi, **8** tram, **9** transport, **10** trolleybus

8.8

1 Moscow, **2** 150 roubles (стоимость рублей: 150)

8.9

1 ИЗМАЙЛОВСКИЙ ПАРК (4), **2** ПУШКИНСКАЯ (7),
3 ЮГО-ЗАПАДНАЯ (10), **4** АЭРОПОРТ (1),
5 ТРЕТЬЯКОВСКАЯ (8)

8.10

ЛАДА

8.11
1 3500 roubles, **2** Arrival (because it is many hours after the train has left Moscow and has arrived in Perm), **3** Train

8.12 Crossword

		¹в	е	р	т	о	л	ё	²т
		а							е
²м	а	г	а	з	и	н			а
		о							т
³б	а	н	³к		⁴с	о	⁴б	о	р
			а				и		
	⁵ж	е	т	о	н		л		
			о				е		
⁶ц	и	р	к		⁷м	е	т	р	о

End-of-unit review questions: 1 бассе́йн, **2** като́к, **3** стоя́нка, **4** собо́р, **5** вокза́л, **6** zebra, zone, zoology; **7** instinct, interest, investment; **8** telescope, tunnel, toaster; **9** shampoo, shock, shorts; **10** energy, exploitation, emotion

---

Unit 9

9.1
1 administrator (receptionist), **2** form, **3** visa, **5** hotel, **8** hotel room, **9** passport, **10** floor/storey

9.2

1 It is central (В центре города).   **2** Name of the metro station to use: «Площадь Александра Невского».

9.3

1 Dostoevsky,   **2** Grant,   **3** No,   **4** $30 (США is the Russian abbreviation for USA),   **5** 1,500,   **6** 23 March 2010

9.4

1 the historical centre,   **2** two minutes' walk,   **3** mini bar, satellite TV, telephone, air-conditioning, en-suite facilities (bath/shower)

9.5

Viktor has got salad and wine instead of omelette and mineral water; Tanya has got mineral water and omelette instead of salad and wine; you have got omelette instead of salad.

9.6

1 breakfast,   **2** a self-service/buffet lunch,   **3** Kremlin and Red Square,   **4** Bolshoi Theatre

9.7

1 reception (administration),   **2** restaurant(s), snack bar(s) and cafeteria(s), bar(s)   **3** 19 November 2009

9.8

1 Cold and snowing,   **2** excellent,   **3** borshsh

End-of-unit review questions: **1** secretarial services,
2 парикмахерская (ремонт means *repair*),   **3** сувенирный киоск (аптечный means *chemist's*, from the noun аптека),
4 theatre tickets,   **5** aerobics, water aerobics, jacuzzi,   **6** billiards, darts, karaoke,   **7** cosmetics and accessories,   **8** massage, manicure, pedicure,   **9** fifteen,   **10** three hundred and twenty

---

Unit 10

10.1

4 basketball

10.2

1 hockey,   **2** Wednesdays and Saturdays,   **3** football

10.3

1 З,   **2** Г,   **3** Б,   **4** Е,   **5** А,   **6** Ж,   **7** И,   **8** В,   **9** К,   **10** Д

10.4
1 Tennis → ТЕННИСНЫЙ КОРТ
2 Figure skating → КАТОК
3 Football → СТАДИОН
4 Swimming → БАССЕЙН
5 Volleyball → ВОЛЕЙБОЛЬНАЯ ПЛОЩАДКА
10.5
1 А, Д, Е, И;　2 Г, Ж, К;　3 Б, В, З
10.6
1 Б,　2 А,　3 university,　4 Saturday

А

> Thursday 10 December
>
> Lecture: 'Computer – friend or enemy?'
>
> (University, 5.30)

Б

> Saturday 19 December
>
> Exhibition: 'The best television serials of our century'
>
> (Library, 09.00–18.00)

10.7
1 tennis and golf,　2 watch films or television,　3 Yalta
10.8
1 Saint Petersburg,　2 Rimsky-Korsakov
10.9
композитор (composer), дирижёр (conductor), симфонии (symphonies), сюиты (suites). Педагог means teacher.
10.10
1 Б,　2 А,　3 В,　4 В,　5 Б,　6 А

10.11
1 hotels, restaurants and casino,   **2** passport or identification
10.12
7 б<u>о</u>дибилдинг (*bodybuilding*), i.e. a sport, leisure activity. The others are:
1 plane,   **2** bus,   **3** motorbike,   **4** bicycle,   **5** helicopter,   **6** tram,
8 metro,   **9** train,   **10** trolleybus
10.13
1 4th floor,   **2** 3rd floor,   **3** 1st floor,   **4** 6th floor,   **5** 2nd floor
10.14
1 Кли<u>е</u>нт В,   **2** Canadian dollars,   **3** 800 roubles   **4** Euros
10.15 Crossword

		¹К	¹Р	Е	²М	Л	Ь			
			О		А		³О			
²Э	Т	А	Ж		Р		³О	Ф	И	⁴С
			Д		Т			И		У
⁴М	У	З	Е	Й				Ц		П
			С					И		
⁵К	⁵А	Р	Т			⁶Б	Р	А	Т	
	В		В					Н		
	Т		⁷О	Р	К	Е	С	Т	⁶Р	
	О								И	
	⁸Р	О	С	С	И	Я			С	

End-of-unit review questions: **1** омл<u>е</u>т,   **2** парк,   **3** снег,
4 <u>а</u>вгуст,   **5** <u>о</u>фис,   **6** b,   **7** c,   **8** a,   **9** c,   **10** a

Vocabulary list

See the comments on gender in Unit 5. The gender of a noun is clear from its ending except in the case of –ь, which can end a masculine or a feminine word. The vocabulary list below tells you which gender the –ь nouns are: (м) indicates a masculine word, and (ж) a feminine one.

а́вгуст *August*
авто́бус *bus*
автомоби́ль (м) *car*
администра́тор *administrator (receptionist)*
а́дрес *address*
апре́ль *April*
аэропо́рт *airport*

ба́бушка *grandmother*
бага́ж *luggage*
бале́т *ballet*
банк *bank*
банки́р *banker*
баскетбо́л *basketball*
бассе́йн *swimming pool*
библиоте́ка *library*
би́знес *business*
биле́т *ticket*
бланк *form*
блин *pancake*
больни́ца *hospital*
борщ *beetroot soup*
брат *brother*
бутербро́д *sandwich*
буты́лка *bottle*
буфе́т *snack bar*

ваго́н *carriage*
велосипе́д *bicycle*
вертолёт *helicopter*
весна́ *spring*
ви́за *visa*
виндсе́рфинг *windsurfing*
вино́ *wine*
вку́сный *delicious*
внук *grandson*
вну́чка *granddaughter*
во́дка *vodka*
вокза́л *railway station*
воскресе́нье *Sunday*
восто́к *east*
всё *all*
вто́рник *Tuesday*
вход *entrance*
вы *you*
вы́бор *choice*
вы́ставка *exhibition*
вы́ход *exit*

галере́я *gallery*
где *where*
геогра́фия *geography*
глаз *eye*
голова́ *head*

го́рничная maid
го́род town
гости́ница hotel
гость (м) guest

дворе́ц palace
де́душка grandfather
дежу́рная lady on duty (on each floor of hotel)
дека́брь (м) December
день (м) day
день рожде́ния birthday
де́ти children
дождь (м) rain
дом house
дочь (ж) daughter
духи́ perfume
дя́дя uncle

ещё still, again, more

жа́рко hot
жена́ wife
жето́н token
журнали́ст journalist

за́втрак breakfast
за́пад west
здесь here
зима́ winter
зуб tooth

игра́ game
игра́ть to play
игро́к player
икра́ caviar
и́ли or
име́ть to have

и́мя name
инжене́р engineer
интере́сно interesting
ию́ль (м) July
ию́нь (м) June

как like, as, how
ката́ние на лы́жах skiing
като́к skating rink
кварти́ра flat
квас kvass (drink made from fermented rye bread)
кино́ (кинотеа́тр) cinema
клие́нт customer
ключ key
кни́га book
когда́ when
компью́тер computer
конфе́ты sweets
конья́к brandy
кот cat
ко́фе coffee
кто who
куда́ where to
купе́ compartment (on train)
ку́хня kitchen, cuisine

ле́то summer
лифт lift

магази́н shop
май May
март March
матч match
мать (ж) mother
маши́на car, machine
ме́сто place, seat
метро́ metro, underground

минеральная вода mineral water

мода fashion

молоко milk

мотоцикл motorbike

муж husband

музей museum

музыка music

мы we

надо it is necessary

нам нравиться we like

начало beginning

номер number, hotel room

нос nose

ноябрь (м) November

обед lunch

обмен валюты currency exchange

обстановка setting, situation

одежда clothes

одним словом in a word

октябрь (м) October

омлет omelette

он he, it (for masculine words)

она she, it (for feminine words)

они they

оно it (for neuter words)

опера opera

осень (ж) autumn

остановка (bus) stop

отец father

отлично excellent

отправление departure

отъезд departure

отчество patronymic

офис office

очень very

памятник monument

парк park

паспорт passport

переход crossing

плавание swimming

платье dress

плохо bad, badly

площадь (ж) square

площадка pitch, ground

поезд train

понедельник Monday

почта post office

праздник festival, holiday, celebration

прибытие arrival

приём reception

пятница Friday

ремонт repair

ресторан restaurant

рисование drawing

Рождество Christmas

Россия Russia

рот mouth

рыбная ловля fishing

самолёт plane

север north

серфинг surfing

сестра sister

служба service

сметана sour cream

смотреть to watch, look at

снег snow

собор cathedral

среда Wednesday

стадион stadium

станция station

стоянка такси taxi rank

студент *student*
суббота *Saturday*
сумка *bag*
суп *soup*
сын *son*
сыр *cheese*

такси *taxi*
там *there*
театр *theatre*
тётя *aunt*
только *only*
трамвай *tram*
транспорт *transport*
троллейбус *trolleybus*
турист *tourist*
ты *you (singular, familiar)*

ужин *supper*
улица *street*
университет *university*
ухо *ear*

фамилия *surname*
февраль (м) *February*
фигурное катание *figure skating*
футбол *football*

химия *chemistry*
хлеб *bread*
хоккей на льду *ice hockey*

холодно *cold*
хорошо *good, well*

цена *price*
центр *centre*
церковь *church*
цирк *circus*
чай *tea*
чемодан *suitcase*
четверг *Thursday*
чтение *reading*

шарф *scarf*
шахматы *chess*

щи *cabbage soup*

экскурсия *excursion*
этаж *floor, storey*

юбка *skirt*
юг *south*

я *I*
я люблю *I like/love*
язык *language, tongue*
январь (м) *January*

Taking it further

Finally, here are details of books and websites to help you develop your command of the Russian language:

Books

The first two books below deal with the language from beginner's to approximately GCSE standard; the others take you to a more advanced level.

Complete Russian, by Daphne West, Hodder & Stoughton, 2010 (ISBN 978 1444 10764 7)

Essential Russian Grammar, by Daphne West, Hodder & Stoughton, 2010 (ISBN 978 1 444 10407 3)

A Comprehensive Russian Grammar, by Terence Wade, Blackwell, 1996 (ISBN 0 631 17502 4)

Using Russian Vocabulary, by Terence Wade, CUP 2009 (ISBN 978 0 521 61236 4)

Using Russian, by Derek Offord and Natalia Goglitsyna, CUP, 2005 (ISBN 978 0 521 54761 1)

Modern Russian Grammar Guide, by John Dunn and Shamil Khairov, Routledge 2009 (ISBN 978 0 415 39750 6)

Tranzit, by Daphne West and Michael Ransome, Bramcote Press, 1996 (ISBN 1 900405 00 8)

Kompas, by Michael Ransome, Daphne West and Rachel Smith, Bramcote Press, 2002 (ISBN 1 900405 08 3)

Navigator, CD-ROM, ed., Michael Ransome, Bramcote Press, 2009 (ISBN 978-1-900405-17-1)

Websites

The following websites will be helpful in finding out more about Russian language, culture and society:

www.ssees.ac.uk/directory.htm

www.crees.bham.ac.uk/links.htm

www.langlink.net

www.gramota.ru

www.rian.ru

www.ucis.pitt.edu/reesweb

www.russophilia.wordpress.com